Introduction

What greater joy is there after a hard week at work than to be able to get out into one's very own garden? Weekend gardening must surely be one of the most popular of pastimes.

Here then is the way to profit from those few heady hours of freedom: a profit that is both pleasurable and material.

By careful planning you can avoid some of the pitfalls which beset the unwary. By sowing flowers from seed you can have colour in your garden all year round with the minimum outlay—a very important consideration if you happen to be setting up home for the first time. By growing your own fruit and vegetables, not only will you be able to live a little better and perhaps a lot longer, you will have the thrill of actually producing your own food.

And to guide you all the basic tasks have been simplified. Here is a step-by-step guide to all the things you are most likely to want to know . . . from how to make compost to how to lay a lawn; from how many fruit bushes to buy to provide for the family to how to deal with pests and diseases if things go wrong. There is help which ranges from choosing trees and shrubs to selecting the most suitable climbers. It is a book in fact which should satisfy both the absolute beginner and expert alike.

The Weekend Gardener has taken account too that most gardens nowadays are very much smaller and that the gardener, however enthusiastic, often has other pressures on his or her time. Yet, even with just a few hours each week, your garden can look really beautiful and as pretty as any of the pictures, in addition to providing an endless challenge to grow something different. With this book at your elbow apricots will vie with apples for your attention; and you will soon be searching out every vacant corner to grow all manner of flowers from anemones to zinnias.

Your garden in your few precious hours is what YOU make of it. But whatever you decide to do, make it fun; for therein lies the magic and the real secret of success.

If this book has but one aim, it is this: to help you to enjoy your weekend . . . gardening!

Max Davidson

Contents

FROM WILDERNESS TO GARDEN

You can transform a bare patch of soil with the subtle blending of grass, colourful flowers and shrubs, a tree and a small pond.

Imagine if you could look out on a garden filled with flowers and surrounded by the greenest grass that you have ever seen. Just think too how marvellous it would be to be able to pick your own fruit and gather your own vegetables, all plump and tasty.

There can be few greater joys in life than gazing with proud satisfaction at one's own well-stocked and cultivated garden. But how does one achieve this happy state of affairs? That is the problem which has beset millions of would-be gardeners for generations.

Nowadays there are so many short cuts that anyone, even with only a couple of hours or so each weekend, can turn a wilderness into his or her idea of the perfect garden.

Above all it is what you want that counts. Gardening should be fun – not a chore. Your ideal might be a garden which has lots of flowers or roses. You may on the other hand expect your garden to make a contribution to the housekeeping budget by supplying you with some of your fruit and vegetables. Alternatively, your prime objective may be to have a safe place for the children to play.

So what do you do if you are starting from scratch with either a new house surrounded by weeds and broken bricks, or an older house with a long-neglected garden?

The right tools
The first step is to get the right tools for the job. With a basic set of good-quality tools

the task may not be that much easier, but it will certainly be more pleasant. Cheap tools are a false economy because they neither last nor do they generally have that correct 'feel' which is so essential to comfortable working. To get the most from your purchases, however, shop around for a discount and preserve the tools by looking after them.

A spade is the basic tool which you will need for digging, but as such activity has put more people off gardening than anything else, do get a spade which you are happy to handle. This generally means one which is fairly light, and, for this reason, your best choice could well be the type called a border spade, rather than the normal digging spade. One with a stainless steel blade may be expensive, but if you have sticky clay soil it will be money well spent in making light work of a heavy task.

A fork is the best tool for breaking up soil which has become consolidated by winter rain. It is also ideal for digging sticky soil or land which is full of stones. In fact, a fork can often do the same tasks as a spade without the same effort.

A rake is vital for levelling the soil and for breaking down the surface to a fine enough texture to enable seeds to be sown.

A hoe does much the same job as a spade and a fork in cultivating the soil. However,

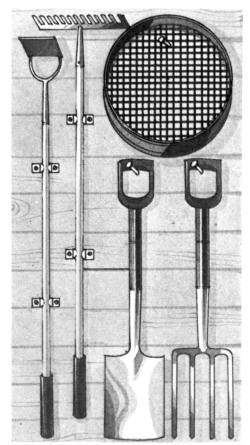

its main function in most gardens is to keep down weeds. There are several kinds of hoe, but the best one for general use is the type with a flat blade called a Dutch hoe. If you can afford it, get one with a stainless steel blade. It takes the backache out of weeding any flowerbed.

A trowel is the implement one uses for planting a wide variety of things – from seedlings to bulbs. Such a tool is often sold as part of a set with a matching hand fork. The latter is ideal for weeding close to plants, where using a Dutch hoe might cause damage.

A garden line, preferably of bright orange polypropylene twine so that it can be seen easily, is vital for 'drawing' those straight lines on your garden.

Shears will be required for cutting hedges – but why not use an electric hedge-cutter, or one powered by a battery? You will also need long-handled shears for trimming the grass at lawn edges. Hand shears, called secateurs, will be necessary for most pruning jobs and for cutting roses and flowers.

A watering can and a hose with some sort of sprinkler are essential garden implements, as we unfortunately cannot rely on natural rainfall providing sufficient water for our plants.

A barrow may be necessary if your garden is large enough, but most people will manage with a plastic bucket.

A pressure sprayer to apply insecticides and fungicides is also important if much of your hard work is not to be wasted.

Finally, what about a mower, you might ask? You will find suggestsions on this subject covered in the chapter on grass.

As well as your basic set of tools there are certain items which are often better hired – for instance, a mechanical cultivator. You could use one in a new garden to rotovate the entire plot and so remove rubble

and loosen the soil compacted by the builders' activities.

Your own plot

However, before you start using any tools, let us take a look at your plot. All loose debris, bricks, large stones, etc., should be collected and put in a pile for use later as hardcore for a patio or under the base of a garden shed. If the plot is at present covered with coarse grass, this can be skimmed off in strips 5cm (2in) thick and stacked carefully so that it will rot down and provide useful compost for feeding the soil later. The quickest way to get the turf to turn into compost is to stack the strips in alternate layers, grass side to grass side, with a sprinkling of sulphate of ammonia between the layers to help the rotting process.

However, if the uncultivated land contains rough weed grasses, such as the one called couch (recognizable by its invasive, white fleshy roots) your best plan is to treat the area first with a selective weedkiller called Dalapon. Woody weeds, such as brambles, nettles, ivy and the sucker growth from old tree trunks, can be simply

Above: Shears are used here to cut a privet hedge, but for extensive hedges an electric or battery powered cutter will save time on this lengthy task.

Left: If the garden is fairly large a wheelbarrow is essential. This is a light-weight barrow with a galvanized steel body and a pneumatic-tyred wheel.

growing strongly, you could still have the plot prepared in time to sow grass seed in summer or early autumn, or lay turf between late August and the end of October.

Often the uncultivated land left by the builders is a mass of annual weeds together with more persistent perennials such as dandelions, thistles and plantains. A satisfactory solution to this problem is to treat the entire area with a weed-killer containing paraquat and diquat, which kills the weeds and yet is rendered harmless on contact with the soil. The dead weed foliage can then be raked up and burned. One application will be sufficient to wipe out most weeds, but others such as dandelions may need a second treatment after a couple of weeks.

All weedkillers are dangerous to the user, children and animals. The instructions provided by the manufacturers must always be followed to the letter. However, used sensibly and carefully they are an invaluable timesaver for the weekend gardener.

Once the rubble and the weeds have been removed, you can draw yourself a plan of action for your garden. Sketch, for instance, where you would like to have a patio to sit and admire the garden when it is completed. Ideally this should be in a sunny position. Decide too about such things as a possible sandpit for the children; a green-

Above: A garden hose is an essential implement for the garden, and it should have some kind of sprinkler attachment. This fitting is known as a fan sprinkler.

Right: Try drawing a plan of your garden with the important features noted, to familiarize yourself with the good and bad points of the area.

eradicated with a brushwood killer. The effect of both these weedkillers persists in the soil for about three months, but if applied in spring, when the weeds are

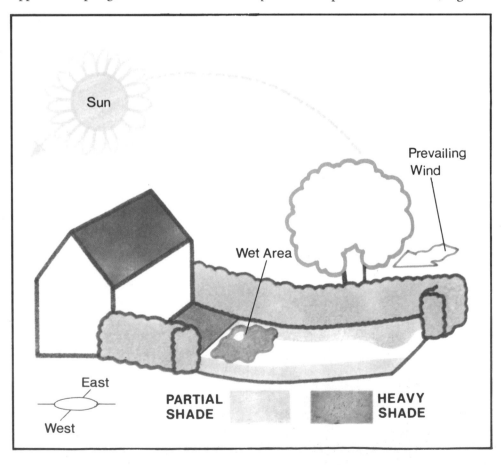

house or cold frame, if one is to be accommodated in the future; a rotary clothes drier; or the position of a pool for plants and fish. How much privacy do you want? Is it necessary to use trees to hide distant objects? Are hedges and fences necessary to protect you from prevailing winds? How much space do you wish to allot to growing vegetables? Once you have asked yourself all these questions you will realize why it is impossible to draw up a masterplan for a garden for others to follow. The truth is that every garden is of necessity different and consequently requires a unique approach. You can get ideas from looking at other gardens and by reading, but in the end you will have to decide on the sort of garden which suits you.

Once you have a rough idea what you want, put your ideas down on paper with a note of the approximate measurements of the various features. By so doing, you will save yourself a great deal of time and energy. For instance, the area which will become a patio should not be dug over at all as such soil disturbance could cause subsidence later. The soil for a lawn need only be turned over to a depth of 23cm (9in) instead of the 30cm (12in) or so required by vegetables, flowers and shrubs.

On most plots it is not necessary to worry about drainage. That should have been attended to by the builders. If it has not, get them back to fix it. Similarly it is a waste of time to attempt to create either artificial levels or to attempt to achieve a lawn with a surface as level as a billiard table. Far better to make use of the natural contours of the land and to achieve the occasional change in level with a retaining wall or a rockery. You could make the latter look as if it might be part of the landscape, instead of simply a mound of earth and stones.

Preparing the soil

Sooner or later, however, you will have to get down to the basic task of digging or forking over the soil. The latter course is often quite acceptable when preparing a lawn. So mark out the different areas with wooden pegs or string to save yourself unnecessary effort.

If the soil is stony, or there is an impervious layer of compacted soil and stones – known as 'hard pan' – just below the surface, normal digging may be impossible and special treatment may be required. The easiest solution is to hire a mechanical cultivator with toughened digging blades to

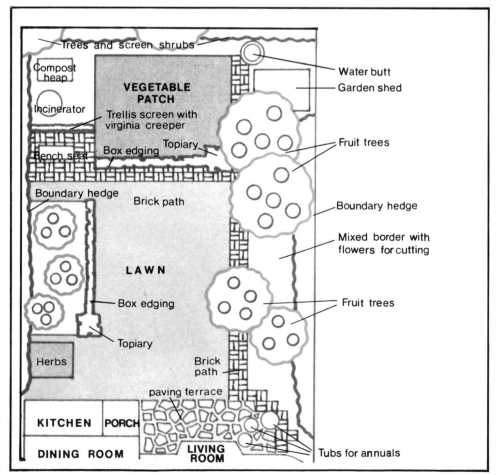

Left: The plan of action for the garden sketched on the previous page. The vegetable patch is in the sunniest part, and a trellis is planned to hide the compost heap. Below: An accurate picture of a garden can be drawn by using graph paper marked out in squares. Use a simple scale (say 1:20) and keep the plan big.

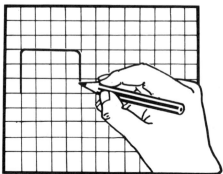

Above: The texture of soil of any type will be improved by the addition of organic matter.

yard). All organic matter, grass cuttings, weeds and certain household waste can go on the heap. The way to produce good compost is to build up the heap in layers of well-mixed material like a sponge cake. Each 23cm (9in) layer should be sprinkled with a compost activator. The time taken for the compost to mature will depend on the season. Unfortunately because of this time variation and the fact that the raw materials, grass cuttings for example, are available more readily during the summer months, two heaps are the minimum required for proper production.

Most new gardens are unlikely to have sufficient organic material to make all the compost that is wanted. So you will have to make use of such substitutes as peat, shredded bark and spent hops to improve the condition of the soil.

Garden compost, as well as improving the physical structure of the soil, provides some plant foods. Peat, shredded bark and spent hops on the other hand provide little plant food at all and, in fact, may actually use up some of the available nitrogen in the soil as they rot down to form humus. Consequently many gardeners make good the soil's need for certain plant foods by adding chemical fertilizers.

Many of the fertilizers are sold in compound form to suit various groups of plants. For instance, a general fertilizer will suit vegetables, fruit and flowers. However, you will get far better results if you use a specific rose fertilizer, containing magnesium and different proportions of the same ingredients as the vegetable fertilizer, on your roses. Similarly lawn fertilizers are often composed of slow-release chemicals which feed the grass over several months and avoid scorching the lawn. However, such fertilizers are expensive and it is wise to buy a simple soil test kit to check what your soil actually requires before you start scattering chemical ferti-

deal with such conditions. The alternative is to fork over the soil to about twice the depth of the fork and leave the soil rough so that it is exposed to the effects of rain, wind and frost.

Heavy clay soils are best dug between late spring and early winter. Never attempt to dig them when they are wet and sticky. You will only make matters worse as well as giving yourself backache. Light soils can be dug at any time.

The texture of a soil, be it sandy, clayey or perfect loam, can be partially determined or improved by the addition of organic matter, which breaks down in the soil to form humus. Humus enables the soil to absorb air and moisture and it ensures that plants will make healthy root systems capable of taking up nourishment. Without humus, the full benefits of fertilizers are wasted.

The vital organic matter can be supplied in several ways. The old-fashioned idea was to use farmyard manure, which is difficult to obtain nowadays, and in any case it is not something which will endear you to your neighbours. Far better to use your own garden compost made in a properly constructed heap. For the majority of gardens the best idea is to buy a couple of plastic or wire compost bins. Alternatively, you could make them from plastic fencing netting and stout posts. The minimum satisfactory size is a cubic metre (about a cubic

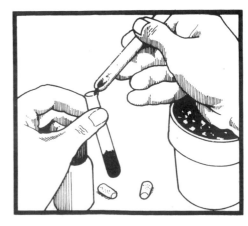

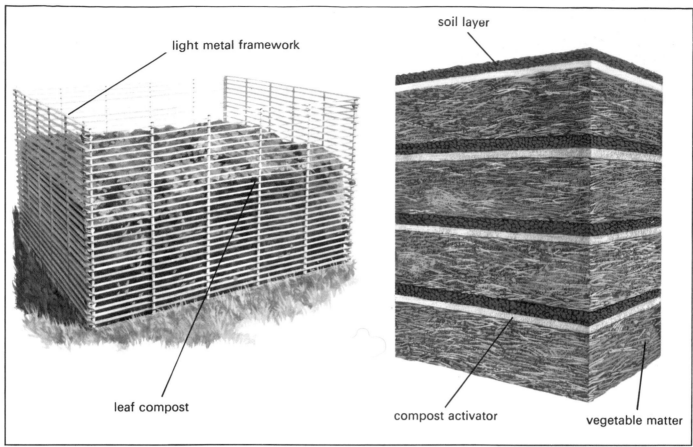

light metal framework

soil layer

leaf compost

compost activator

vegetable matter

lizer around the garden. Such a test kit will also tell you if your soil is 'alkaline' and has plenty of calcium, which is normally added when necessary in the form of lime. It is also possible that the test will reveal that little calcium is present and your soil is 'acid'. This particular piece of information can prove vital in determining the type of flowers and shrubs which you will be able to grow in your garden, because, broadly speaking, there are those plants which like lime and those which hate it, and in between a great number of plants which tolerate soil conditions normally referred to as 'neutral'.

It used to be the rule that deciduous trees and shrubs were planted any time between early November and the end of March, provided the soil was not water-logged or frozen over. Nowadays with garden centres selling trees and shrubs, container grown, you can plant at virtually any time of the year. What a boon this is for the busy weekend gardener who may not have the time to pick and choose when to plant. Evergreen trees and shrubs are now nearly always sold in containers, so they too can be planted when it suits you best. Surely it is not possible to get any more instant gardening than that?

Finishing the construction work
However, before you get around to doing any planting the chances are that you will wish to finish the construction work. The biggest job is usually that of laying a patio

Above: Garden compost should be made in a properly constructed heap enclosed in a frame and built up in layers.

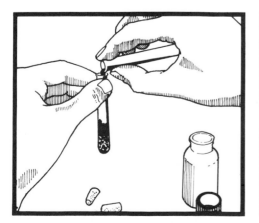

Left: A simple soil-test kit checks exactly what type of soil a garden has. This information is vital to determine what the soil requires in the way of fertilizer and lime, and also what kind of plants will grow happily in that soil.

Above: This patio has been thoughtfully laid out in contrasting shades, using varying shapes of concrete slabs and paving stones with round pebbles to fill in the small spaces.

Below: A fence bedecked with climbing roses makes an effective backing to this border, which includes a low hedge of lavender.

from concrete slabs. There are many shades available and with care you can lay a patio as attractive as one constructed from genuine stone. You can lay a straight-forward checkerboard pattern or, by using slabs of different sizes, produce a random pattern. In any case, never lay slabs larger than 60cm by 60cm (24in by 24in) as they are almost impossibly heavy to handle on your own.

Before ordering any materials, draw yourself a plan of the area to scale, perhaps 2cm to 60cm (1in to 24in). You can then work out how many slabs you require. Unless you can be absolutely certain that the area where you intend to lay your patio contains undisturbed soil, your best bet is to excavate it to a depth of 15cm (6in) and to fill it with 7.5cm to 10cm (3in to 4in) of rubble topped with a level bed of sand. Achieving this level bed can be done by means of wooden pegs hammered into the ground and linked with taut strings, which can be checked with a spirit level. Start laying the slabs in the corners of the given area, tap them lightly into position with a piece of board, check them with a spirit level and ensure that they are in alignment with the strings. After the patio has been laid for a week, brush a mixture of sand and cement between the joints and wash this in. This latter operation can be repeated as often as is necessary.

The same technique can also be applied to making paths from paving slabs. You could also consider using bricks laid in a bed of sand. Bricks, or small interlocking concrete blocks, make very attractive paths as well as sturdy and beautiful patios.

Many gardens are too small to need paths. Often a few stepping stones is all that is required to reach the vegetable plot, greenhouse or compost bin. Such 'stepping stones' can be made by sinking small slabs into the lawn. Look out for circular and hexagonal slabs as these can produce a pleasing pattern.

The next most important construction job in the garden is putting up fencing. Most gardens already have some sort of boundary fence, but often additional fencing is required to ensure privacy or to shelter the garden from chilling winds. The best course is to buy your fence panels ready made once you have decided on the size and type you require. Any fence, of course, is only as good as the posts supporting it. Therefore your posts should be set in concrete, or into metal post holders which have previously been sunk into the ground.

For many people a hedge still makes the most effective boundary. You can choose between a low hedge, which simply marks out the territory of your front garden, and a tall hedge which provides shelter and a screen from prying eyes.

For a small, front garden hedge you could choose berberis, lavender or rosemary. At the back of the house you might have beech which does well on heavy wet soils; hawthorn, which is resistant to animals; or a floribunda rose such as Queen Elizabeth. All of these three lose their leaves in winter. If you want a conifer hedge which is extremely fast growing and yet responds readily to clipping, grow *Cupressocyparis leylandii*. Other good evergreen hedging shrubs are escallonia, which is resistant to sea gales, golden privet and cotoneaster.

When you order the shrubs, the nurseryman will tell you how many you need to a running metre (yard). Before planting any hedge the soil must be prepared by forking in some compost, or peat, and then top dressed with granular general fertilizer. Most hedges will require cutting at least once a year: late spring for the Cupressocyparis, escallonia, lavender, rosemary and Queen Elizabeth rose; summer for the beech, hawthorn, berberis and cotoneaster, and whenever necessary for the golden privet.

Finally what about a garden pond with flowers and fish? Building such a pond used to be a major undertaking when concrete was needed to line the pool. Now you can simply scoop a hole in the ground, line that with soft sand and then install a ready-made glass fibre pool. However, before making a start on your pool do ensure that it will be in a position which gets sunshine for at least half a day and that it is away from overhanging trees, which will inevitably drop their leaves.

By far the cheapest and best method of making a pool is to use a liner of PVC or butyl which acts as a watertight envelope when placed in a hole in the ground. The great advantage of this method of pool construction is that you can decide exactly the shape you wish your pool to be. There is no need, incidentally, for a pool to be deep – 45cm to 60cm (18in to 24in) is sufficient for the majority of plants and fish. You could also install a submersible pump to power a fountain or to provide a waterfall of water from pools at different levels.

All the equipment, plants and fish are best obtained from a specialist water gardening firm which will ensure that you can stock your pool at the most suitable time of year.

Water in the garden is so soothing and restful, whether murmuring and splashing or simply the home for some colourful fish. A pool too makes the ideal spot to laze beside on a hot summer's day while thinking about what you ought to be doing in the garden. Yet doesn't planning ahead make you positively look forward to weekends in the garden?

A pool in a sunny part of the garden is a favourite feature. Even if it is very small it can be a restful sight and a focal point for the garden.

WHERE THE GRASS IS GREENER

Regular mowing and the elimination of pests and weeds will help to acheive a lovely lawn which is restful to the eye and the perfect foil for brilliantly coloured flowers.

A beautifully mown, healthy lawn is often the first thing that other people notice about your garden, and it is no wonder that gardeners take so much time and trouble to attain an immaculate green 'carpet'. Green grass is restful to the eye in summer; it provides the perfect foil for brilliantly coloured flowers and it enhances your home. In winter a well-tended lawn is often the only relief from that season's gloom.

Producing a lovely lawn was never easy, but thanks to modern gardening aids even the weekend gardener can with very little effort achieve perfection. The key to success is having properly prepared soil right from the start. One tends to overlook the fact that grass is a plant which needs the same feeding and care as any other if it is to grow well. Regular mowing and the elimination of pests and weeds also help to achieve the desired result.

The first decision people with new gardens have to take is whether to make a lawn from seed or turf. Seed is the cheapest and it enables you to suit the actual grasses to your soil and purpose. You could use a fine mixture of seed for a front lawn which would get very little 'wear'. Such a mixture of dwarf grasses would produce a lawn with the appearance of a bowling green. The snags with this type of grass mixture are that the lawn must be kept trimmed at least once a week and will require regular feeding, and possibly watering, in dry spells.

By far the most popular lawn for the average garden is the kind which has been produced by sowing a mixture of fine and hard-wearing broad leaved grasses. This type of lawn looks good and yet has the ability to resist wear lacking in the finer lawn.

Next there is the kind of grass mixture which contains a high proportion of broad leaved grasses, including perennial rye-grass. This type of lawn will never be beautiful, but it is sufficiently hard wearing to resist the activities of energetic dogs and children playing. Such grass also grows quickly and it is the best choice for poor, clay soils if you do not feel like spending the money to make the necessary improvements for a finer lawn seed mixture.

Turf provides the quickest usable lawn, but unless it can be purchased specially grown from seed it could provide you with a considerable number of problems. Avoid, if possible, offers of meadow turf which contains undesirable grasses and weeds.

Preparing the soil

Whatever method you intend to employ to make a lawn the soil must be thoroughly prepared. After the site has been cleared of all rubble and weeds, rotovate the soil or dig it over to a depth of 23cm (9in) as described in the previous chapter. If your soil is light, peat should be forked in at the rate of 3kg per square metre ($5\frac{1}{2}$lb per square yd) to help it retain moisture. If your soil is heavy, then coarse, gritty sand or fine gravel should be incorporated to loosen the texture and help the drainage.

When the soil is sufficiently dry to walk on without its sticking to your boots, the surface should be levelled by raking and treading with your heels. Continue this raking and treading until the soil has a fine crumbly appearance and all hollows have

Below left: Rake the surface of the soil until it has a fine crumbly appearance.
Below right: Mark the plot into even strips and this will ensure accurate sowing.

been eliminated. Do not worry overmuch about stones – only remove those larger than a golf ball. It is a mistake to sieve the soil finely as after heavy rain you will be left with a sea of mud.

Sowing

Grass seed can be sown at any time between April and the end of September. August and September sowings have the advantage that the soil is warm and the seed germinates rapidly. Fewer weeds grow during the autumn and winter and there is usually enough rain. So by the following spring, a late summer or early autumn sown lawn is thick and lush. April, however, may be the best month for sowing in northern districts where the cold and lack of daylight in autumn and winter lead to poor grass growth.

A day or two before sowing (or turfing) apply a general fertilizer over the site at the rate of 56g per square metre (2oz per square yard) and rake in lightly. For soils of an acid character lime should be applied appropriately a week or two before grass sowing. For accurate sowing mark out the plot with long bamboo canes or string laid in one metre (yard) squares to help achieve an even application of the grass seed. Then sow the seed at the rate of 42g to 56g per square metre ($1\frac{1}{2}$oz to 2oz per square yard).

After sowing, the soil can be very lightly raked, but on no account should the seed be buried, otherwise it will fail to germinate.

Grass seed is generally sold treated with a chemical making it unpalatable to birds, but harmless to children and pets. On warm dry days sparrows may attempt to take dust baths on your newly sown lawn. The

Caring for the lawn: a crumbling or worn edge can be renovated by lifting a square of turf and reversing it so that the thin grass can recover and the thicker grass can take the wear of the constant traffic.

solution is either to use black cotton threaded around small stakes and covering the entire area, or to keep the soil damp by sprinkling it with water. In any case lawns sown from May to August may need to be watered regularly to ensure germination, which under normal conditions takes one to two weeks, as a sudden drought can kill the seedlings before their roots have developed properly.

Cutting

Once the new grass has grown to a height of 5cm (2in) it can be cut lightly to reduce its length to 2.5cm (1in). This first cut should be made while the grass is perfectly dry, and the clippings should be collected in the mower's grass box or gently raked off the new lawn using a spring toothed rake. On subsequent cuttings the mower can be set progressively lower until you reach a height of 1.25cm ($\frac{1}{2}$in) for front lawns and 2cm ($\frac{3}{4}$in) for back garden lawns which have to take more wear. The golden rule for all lawns is to cut at least once a week and never to wait for the grass to get over long before cutting it.

Turfing

Before turfing, prepare the soil in the same way as for sowing (see above). Turf is usually supplied cut in 30cm by 90cm (1ft by 3ft) strips. When turfing, start at one end of the site and lay in straight rows, staggering the turfs in alternate rows like bricks in a wall. However avoid using small sections at the edges where they are easily disturbed. Stand on a plank to prevent the soil becoming consolidated as you work. Check too that each turf lies level with its neighbour and make the necessary ad-

justment by adding soil or removing it from under the turf. As you proceed, beat down the turfs lightly with the back of a spade to ensure firm contact with the soil. Once all the turfs are laid, fill in all the cracks between them with a mixture of moist peat and good soil to encourage the turfs to knit together.

The newly laid lawn will require to be watered frequently if the weather is dry. For this reason, although turf can be laid at any time, best results are obtained in early spring and autumn.

Caring for the lawn

Once you have a lawn you will naturally wish to give it the care it deserves. The most important operation is cutting the grass. There is a very wide choice of mowers available with either cylinder or rotary blades. Most mowers now are powered, even those for very small lawns, so that grass cutting is no more difficult than vacuum-cleaning a carpet. Your best plan is to choose a mower which picks up the grass, as grass clippings left on a lawn are easily carried by feet into the home. Those much admired stripes on lawns are produced by mowers with rear rollers, which also enable you to cut right up to lawn edges. Rotary mowers give best results with less than perfect grass. They are also ideal in areas of high rainfall where the grass often has to be cut while it is wet. Cylinder mowers give the finest possible finish on ornamental lawns.

Regular mowing encourages the finer grasses and reduces the number of coarse grasses in the lawn. Mow at least once a week between April and October and occasionally in mild winters if possible. Always vary your direction of mowing over the year to ensure even cutting. Most lawns should never be cut any shorter than 2cm ($\frac{3}{4}$in) as 'scalping' inevitably means a miserable brown lawn for much of the summer.

Mowing provides for the main part of lawn care, but the overall effect can be ruined if the edges are untidy. You can do away with the chore of trimming edges by edging the lawn with small paving slabs or bricks set slightly lower than the turf. If you do have edges to trim, however, keep them neat by placing a board at the edge of the lawn and by cutting the turf once a year with either your spade or a lawn edging tool. Then every time you cut the grass, trim the ragged edges with edging shears.

If you continue to cut your grass without feeding it, it soon becomes pale, weedy and full of moss. Regular feeding is consequently vital. Ideally you should use a lawn fertilizer in April and in September. Fertilizer can be applied by hand, but better distribution can be obtained if you use a special lawn spreader.

Even a lawn which is cut regularly tends to form a mat of dead foliage on the surface which resists the passage of air and water to the grass roots. The name usually given to this matted grass is 'thatch'. In spring and autumn the dead matter should be removed from the lawn with a spring toothed rake. If the lawn has had a lot of use

Above left: The first cutting of a newly sown lawn should be done lightly with garden shears.
Above right: Any perennial weeds which appear should be removed by hand.

in the summer, it may also have become compacted with the tell-tale signs of moss starting to grow. The cure is to spike the lawn all over to a depth of 10cm (4in) with your garden fork. Then after spiking improve the texture of the soil by top-dressing the lawn with fine moss peat. Such a top dressing is also useful in filling any hollows. However, do not apply the dressing so thickly that it smothers the grass.

Feeding generally helps to avoid most lawn problems, but occasionally after a very wet winter following a dry summer, moss can invade a lawn. You can either remove this by raking and feeding or you can kill the moss with a fertilizer containing iron sulphate or a special moss killer, watered on to the lawn.

If your lawn has uneven bumps, the answer is to lift the turf and remove some of the soil from underneath. Never roll a lawn. Rolling may be fine for bowling greens and cricket pitches but it can prove disastrous in the garden. A crumbling lawn edge can be repaired in autumn by lifting a square of turf at the lawn edge and reversing it so that the broken edge is towards the centre of the lawn.

Worms in lawns produce unsightly casts on the lawn in autumn and winter. The best way of dealing with them is to scatter some dry peat on the lawn then to brush this off together with the worm casts.

Weeds are the most common problem with lawns. Selective weedkillers, either allied to fertilizers, or separately in liquid form, will kill all lawn weeds when applied as instructed by the manufacturers. They are most effective between May and September while the weeds are growing strongly. However, they must never be used on lawns less than a year old. Similarly the clippings from a lawn treated with weed-killer must be kept separate from other organic matter and composted for six months before they can be used as part of the compost.

Month by month guide to a better lawn:

January: Remove the last of the previous autumn's fallen leaves.

February: Remove worm casts and cut the grass if necessary.

March: Rake the grass with a spring toothed rake and cut.

April: Apply a lawn fertilizer and increase the frequency of grass cutting.

May: Inspect for weeds and apply a weedkiller if necessary.

June, July and August: Cut at least once a week. Persistent weeds such as yarrow may need a second application of selective weedkiller.

September: Remove worm casts if necessary, use lawn fertilizer and reduce frequency of mowing.

October: Rake the lawn with a spring toothed rake, spike with a fork and top dress with fine moss peat.

November: Remove any debris such as fallen leaves.

December: Keep off the grass if it is wet or frozen! Following a mild autumn you may have to give the lawn its final cut of the year.

Below left: Work in a top-dressing to improve the texture of the lawn.
Below right: If the dressing is too thick it will smother the lawn, so the surplus should be brushed off.

ADDING THE COLOUR

Colour can be acheived all the year round with annuals and perennials, climbers and small shrubs, all planted thoughtfully as in this cottage garden.

Below: Many shrubs need no pruning at all and planting borders with this in mind can be a great time-saver. Here azaleas give a marvellous splash of colour to a terraced garden.
Opposite page, top: Calendulas—sometimes called marigolds—have orange daisy-like flowers and will do well in light shade on poor soil.
Opposite page, bottom: Alyssum is a good edging plant and is grown for its sweetly-scented white flowers.

Planting trees, shrubs and flowers in a garden is a bit like furnishing a room – it is all a matter of taste. So there is no reason why your ideas should not be as good as anyone else's. Mistakes will be made, but these are usually put right easily. The best idea is to experiment until you find the right 'mix' for your garden.

The quickest way to transform any patch of bare soil into a blaze of colour is to plant some annuals. These are plants, as the name suggests, which complete their life cycle in one short season. Annuals are sown outdoors, where they flower in spring, and at this time they beat every other plant for the sheer number of flowers which they produce.

Annuals sown outdoors are classified by seedsmen as 'hardy'. Others which need a spot of warmth to help germinate the seed are called 'half-hardy'.

You do not need a heated greenhouse to raise half-hardy annuals from seed. Most of them can be grown very satisfactorily on a sunny window sill indoors. Ideally you should have a cold frame, or a couple of large cloches to harden off the plants in late spring before planting them in the garden in late May or early June when all risk of frost has passed and they are acclimatized to being outside.

Biennials are like annuals in that they generally flower once then die. However, unlike annuals, they take two years to flower instead of one. Biennials are best sown in a small seed bed outdoors in June or July and transplanted to their final quarters in the autumn.

Some herbaceous, or perennial plants, such as lupins and columbines can also be raised in this way with a considerable saving in money.

Annuals

Good soil preparation is important with all kinds of annuals. Fork over the ground in early spring to a depth of 23cm (9in) and work in some moist peat. Then about two weeks before sowing, scatter some general fertilizer over the soil at the rate of 56g per square metre (2oz per square yard) and rake this in, so that at the time you are able to produce a fine bed of soil for the seed.

Below are just some of the annuals which you could grow.

Alyssum
Height and spread: 10cm by 30cm (4in by 12in).
Colour of flowers: White, pink or lilac.
When to sow: April and May.
Position: Full sun in ordinary soil.
Growing tip: Dead-head with scissors to ensure continuous flowering.

Calendula
Height and spread: 23cm to 60cm by 15cm to 30cm (9in to 24in by 6in to 12in).
Colour of flowers: Orange, yellow, apricot and cream.
When to sow: March and April.
Position: Sun or light shade on poor soil.
Growing tip: Remove the first flowers to make the plants bushy.

Candytuft
Height and spread: 23cm to 43cm by 15cm to 43cm (9in to 18in by 6in to 18in).
Colour of flowers: Mixed, but mainly red and carmine.
When to sow: March to May.
Position: Full sun on poor soil.
Growing tip: Good choice for city gardens.

Clarkia
Height and spread: 43cm by 30cm (18in by 12in).
Colour of flowers: Purple, red, pink and white.
When to sow: March and April.
Position: Full sun on ordinary soil.
Growing tip: Support plants with twiggy sticks and twine.

Cornflower
Height and spread: 30cm to 90cm by 23cm to 60cm (12in to 3ft by 9in to 2ft).

Colour of flowers: Blue, red, pink and white.
When to sow: April and May.
Position: Full sun on ordinary soil.
Growing tip: Support tall plants and remove dead heads with scissors.

Eschscholzia (Californian poppy)
Height and spread: 15cm to 38cm by 15cm (6in to 15in by 6in).
Colour of flowers: Yellow, pink, red, orange and scarlet.
When to sow: March to May.
Position: Full sun on poor soil.
Growing tip: Allow plants to self-seed as they will flower again in the autumn.

Godetia
Height and spread: 23cm to 60cm by 15cm to 30cm (9in to 24in by 6in to 12in).
Colour of flowers: Red, pink, orange and white.
When to sow: March and April.
Position: Full sun on light soil.
Growing tip: Allow to self-seed for Autumn flowers.

Gypsophila
Height and spread: 23cm to 45cm by 45cm (9in to 18in by 18in).
Colour of flowers: White or pink.
When to sow: March and April.
Position: Full sun on ordinary soil.
Growing tip: If the soil is 'acid', add a little lime before sowing.

Helichrysum
('everlasting' straw flower)
Height and spread: 45cm to 90cm by 23cm to 30cm (18in to 3ft by 9in to 12in).

Above: Godetia makes showy flowers in borders or central flower-beds.
Right: Eschscholzia produces semi-double flowers in various shades. This Californian poppy will flower over a long period of time.

Colour of flowers: Pink, crimson, yellow, orange and white.
When to sow: March to May.
Position: Full sun on ordinary soil.
Growing tip: Cut the flowers before they are fully open. Then dry, hanging upside down in an airing cupboard or another warm place, for winter indoor decoration.

Larkspur
Height and spread: 23cm to 90cm by 30cm to 38cm (9in to 3ft by 12in to 15in).
Colour of flowers: Blue, red and white.
When to sow: March and April.
Position: Full sun on ordinary soil.
Growing tip: Remove flowers as they fade.

Mignonette
Height and spread: 30cm to 38cm by 15cm to 23cm (12in to 15in by 6in to 9in).
Colour of flowers: Yellow tinged with red, red and green.
When to sow: March and April.
Position: Full sun on rich, alkaline soil.
Growing tip: If soil is acid, add lime before sowing.

Nasturtium
Height and spread: 15cm to 2m by 15cm to 60cm (6in to 6ft by 6in to 24in).
Colour of flowers: Yellow, pink, red, orange and various other shades.
When to sow: April and May.
Position: Full sun in poor soil.
Growing tip: The climbing varieties are splendid for concealing ugly fences.

Nigella (love-in-a-mist)
Height and spread: 23cm to 45cm by 23cm to 30cm (9in to 18in by 9in to 12in).
Colour of flowers: Blue, pink, white, red, mauve and purple.
When to sow: March and April.
Position: Full sun in ordinary soil.
Growing tip: Dead-head with scissors to ensure continuous bloom.

Sunflower
Height and spread: 60cm to 3m by 30cm to 60cm (24in to 10ft by 12in to 24in).
Colour of flowers: Yellow, primrose, bronze and maroon.
When to sow: April.
Position: Full sun in rich, well-drained soil.
Growing tip: Place three seeds at each flowering position and thin to one plant later.

Sweet peas
Height and spread: 60cm to 2m by 60cm to 90cm (24in to 6ft by 24in to 3ft).
Colour of flowers: White, cream, pink, red and lavender.
When to sow: April.
Position: Full sun in well-prepared rich soil.
Growing tip: Remove faded blooms and do not allow the plants to produce seed pods. Water well in dry spells.

Above: The sweet-pea is a constant favourite both for its many delicate shades and lovely perfume which make it especially pleasing as a cut flower. This is a successful flower to train on a frame-work or trellis.
Left: Nigella, or Love-in-a-mist, gets its name from the way the feathery leaves surround the delicate blue flowers.

23

Half-hardy annuals

Half-hardy annuals provide some of the most brilliant colours and most beautiful flowers in the garden. They are marvellous for filling in bare patches, and some are splendid for window boxes, tubs and hanging baskets.

With modern peat-based composts the raising of half-hardy annuals could not be simpler. All you need is a seed tray, some compost and a packet of seeds. Fill the tray with compost, firm it gently and water it lightly if necessary to make it moist but not wet. Then sprinkle the seeds as thinly as possible over the compost. Little seeds, the size of pepper grains, should not be covered with compost. Larger seeds may need to be covered to a depth of 6mm ($\frac{1}{4}$in). The next step is to cover the tray with a piece of polythene to retain moisture and prevent the compost from drying out. Since most half-hardy annuals require a temperature of around 18°C (64°F) to germinate the seed, place the tray in a warm, dark spot.

Inspect the tray from time to time, and as soon as the first specks of life appear, move the tray and seedlings to a warm, sunny window sill. When the seedlings have produced 'true' leaves, in addition to

Raising half-hardy annuals is a simple task and they need very little attention. Here, two colourful species, antirrhinums and African marigolds combined with variegated maize make a bright summer-bedding display. Above right: Nowadays dahlias need no specialized attention and will flower profusely over several months.

their oval seedling leaves, it is time to transplant them to seedtrays containing a peat-based potting compost.

The trays should be prepared as for sowing seed and each little seedling should be 'pricked out' and planted gently about 5cm (2in) apart from its neighbours. Small seedlings such as lobelia can be pricked out in groups of three or four. For this job you can either use a pencil or the blade of a small screwdriver. It is important to hold the plants lightly by their seedling leaves to prevent damage.

After transplanting, the seedlings can be watered from a watering can fitted with a fine rose, and the seed tray placed on a window ledge out of direct sun for a day or two until the seedlings take firm root again.

By early May you can put the seed trays outdoors by day to acclimatize the plants to outdoor living, taking them indoors again at night. If you have a garden frame or cloches, the seed trays could be placed under them for protection until the risk of frost has passed and the plants can be set out in their flowering positions in soil prepared in the same way as for sowing hardy annuals.

Below are a few of the many half-hardy annuals that you could grow.

Antirrhinum
Height and spread: 15cm to 60cm by 23cm to 30cm (6in to 24in by 9in to 12in).
Colour of flowers: White, yellow, orange, red and mauve.
When to sow: February and March.
Position outdoors: Sunny in ordinary soil.
Growing tip: Pinch out centre of plants to make them bushy.

Aster
Height and spread: 23cm to 60cm by 30cm to 45cm (9in to 24in by 12in to 18in).
Colour of flowers: Available in all colours.
When to sow: March and April.
Position outdoors: Sunny, sheltered and well-drained soil.
Growing tip: Remove dead flowers to prolong the floral display.

Dahlia
Height and spread: 30cm to 60cm by 30cm to 60cm (12in to 24in by 12in to 24in).
Colour of flowers: Yellow, pink, red, lilac, white and mixed shades.
When to sow: March and April.
Position outdoors: Sunny or light shade in soil enriched with compost.
Growing tip: Water freely in dry spells.

Lobelia
Height and spread: 10cm to 15cm by 15cm to 30cm (4in to 6in by 6in to 12in).
Colour of flowers: Shades of blue, white and red.

Below: Asters, for very little effort, will produce a bank of colour in a late summer border.

When to sow: February and March.
Position outdoors: Partial shade in rich soil.
Growing tip: Superb plants for window boxes and hanging baskets.

Marigolds (French and African)
Height and spread: 15cm to 75cm by 15cm to 45cm (6in to 30in by 6in to 18in).
Colour of flowers: Many shades of yellow, orange and maroon.
When to sow: March.
Position outdoors: Sunny aspect on well-drained rich soil.
Growing tip: Dead-heading encourages growth of the plant and more flowers will be produced.

Nemesia
Height and spread: 23cm to 45cm by 10cm to 15cm (9in to 18in by 4in to 6in).
Colour of flowers: Blue, various bi-colours and mixed.
When to sow: February to April.
Position outdoors: Sunny and slightly acid soil.
Growing tip: Cut back the plants after flowering to promote fresh growth and more flowers.

Petunia
Height and spread: 15cm to 30cm by 30cm (6in to 12in by 12in).
Colour of flowers: All colours and some bicolours.
When to sow: January to March.
Position outdoors: Sheltered and sunny, and ordinary soil.
Growing tip: Excellent for window boxes and hanging baskets. The plants are among the best at surviving droughts.

Phlox
Height and spread: 15cm to 30cm by 23cm (6in to 12in by 9in).
Colour of flowers: All colours in various shades.
When to sow: March and April.
Position outdoors: Sunny on well-drained soil.
Growing tip: Feed with liquid fertilizer in summer to promote more flowers.

Salvia
Height and spread: 23cm to 45cm by 23cm to 45cm (9in to 18in by 9in to 18in).
Colour of flowers: Red, pink scarlet, purple and lavender.
When to sow: January to March.
Position outdoors: Sunny on ordinary soil.

Below left: These handsome petunias vary widely in colour and marking and make extremely effective displays in late summer and early autumn.
Below right: Nemesia makes an attractive border in its wide range of colours.

Left: There are many different species of salvia. This one—the thistle salvia—is a dramatic spiky plant with bluish-purple flowers. Above: This beautiful zinnia is named 'Persian Carpet'.

Growing tip: Pinch off the tops when the plants are about 8cm (3in) high to make them bushy.

Zinnia
Height and spread: 23cm to 75cm by 15cm to 30cm (9in to 30in by 6in to 12in).

Colour of flowers: Various, but mainly shades of yellow, red and orange.

When to sow: March and April.

Position outdoors: Sunny and sheltered in rich soil.

Growing tip: Dead-heading promotes further flowers.

Biennials

The foxglove is a tall graceful flower which is useful for borders and wild gardens.

Biennials are especially useful in the garden because they often flower early in the year. Most can be sown in a small seed bed in a partly shaded position. Some, like the primrose, are better started off in seed compost indoors and then transplanted to a small nursery bed, before being moved to their final position in the autumn. Here then are some biennials which are easy to grow and provide plenty of colour.

Forget-me-not
Height and spread: 15cm to 30cm by 15cm to 23cm (6in to 12in by 6in to 9in).
Colour of flowers: Several shades of blue.
When to sow: May to July.
Final position: Partial shade in soil enriched with peat. .
Growing tip: Grow together with tulips and wallflowers for a dazzling display.

Foxglove
Height and spread: 90cm to 150cm by 45cm (3ft to 5ft by 18in).
Colour of flowers: White, cream, pink, apricot, yellow, red and purple.
When to sow: May and June.
Final position: Light shade and moisture-retaining soil.
Growing tip: Put a layer of moist peat around the roots of the plants to stop them from wilting.

Hollyhock
Height and spread: 90cm to 180cm by 30cm to 45cm (3ft to 6ft by 12in to 18in).
Colour of flowers: Red, pink, white and yellow.
When to sow: May and June.
Final position: Sunny, sheltered, rich soil.
Growing tip: Dead-head to prevent self-seeding.

Pansy

Height and spread: 15cm to 23cm by 23cm to 30cm (6in to 9in by 9in to 12in).
Colour of flowers: Most colours, single shades and blotched.
When to sow: June and July.
Final position: Sun or partial shade on good soil.
Growing tip: Dead-head regularly to maintain flowering.

Primrose (including Polyanthus)

Height and spread: 15cm to 30cm by 23cm (6in to 12in by 9in).
Colour of flowers: All shades, both mixed and single.
When to sow: Indoors in April or May and move to a shaded spot in July.
Final position: Sun or partial shade and soil enriched with peat.
Growing tip: Water plants frequently in dry weather.

Sweet William

Height and spread: 30cm to 60cm by 23cm (12in to 24in by 9in).
Colour of flowers: Pink, red and white.
When to sow: May and June.
Final position: Sunny and ordinary soil, preferably containing a little lime.
Growing tip: Remove all faded flowers.

Wallflower

Height and spread: 23cm to 60cm by 23cm (9in to 24in by 9in).
Colour of flowers: Yellow, orange, red, russet and purple.
When to sow: May and June.
Final position: Sunny and any well-drained soil.
Growing tip: Pinch off the growing points of the plants at 15cm (6in) to encourage side-shoots. Acid soils are best with a top dressing of lime at the rate of 112g per square metre (4oz to a sq yd).

Below: The pansy, an attractive bedding plant, will do well in an open position with some shade from the mid-day sun. This red is the rarest tint in the whole range of colour to be found in the pansy.

Above: There is a good range of winter-flowering pansies which will bloom from March onwards.
Left: The primrose is a woodland plant, flowering in spring in cool, moist areas of the garden.

Perennials

Annuals and biennials fill in the gaps in the garden and are splendid for a splash of spring and summer colour. However, we also need perennials to produce a more permanent background of colour, mainly in spring and autumn. The soil for perennial, or herbaceous, plants as they are also called, must be well prepared as the plants generally remain undisturbed for a number of years.

The positions for the plants should be dug over thoroughly during the winter and the soil enriched with compost. Before the plants are set in place in March, the soil should be well broken down with a fork.

There are hundreds of different plants available from which you can make your choice. Here are a number of brief selections for an assortment of situations.

Plants which thrive in shade
Anemone (pink or white flowers); acanthus (mauve flowers); astilbe (pink, red or white flowers); helleborus (pink, white, purple or maroon flowers, depending on the species); lamium (inconspicuous flowers, but beautiful white leaves) and the ornamental grasses: avena, carex and miscanthus.

Plants which like sunshine
Achillea (yellow or white flowers); aster (blue, pink, red or violet flowers); chrysanthemum – the 'Shasta Daisies' – (white flowers); columbine (many rich colours); delphinium (blue shades, white and pink flowers); iris (flowers of all colours); lupins (flowers of most colours) and sedum (pink, red or yellow flowers).

Plants which need no staking
Doronicum (yellow flowers); day lilies (flowers with several colour combinations); erigeron (blue, violet and pink flowers); euphorbia (green, yellow or orange flowers); peony (pink, red or white flowers) and salvia (violet, blue or pink flowers).

Plants with beautiful leaves
Bergenia (red, purplish or bronze evergreen leaves); acanthus (dark green deeply divided leaves); astilbe (fern like leaves); hosta (leaves in bluish green and combinations of green, cream, yellow and white); lamium (white fleecy leaves); peony (green or bronze divided foliage) and ornamental grasses (leaves of blue, grey, silver, gold, purple and various stripes).

Plants with a pleasing perfume

Lily-of-the-valley, dianthus, water lily, iris, and viola.

Plants which grow well in damp positions

Astilbe; gunnera (ornamental foliage resembling rhubarb); helleborus (white, apple green, pink or purple flowers); primula (orange, scarlet, violet, yellow, mauve or purple flowers, depending on the species); sidalcea (crimson, pink or salmon flowers) and trollius (bright orange or deep yellow flowers).

Plants which cover the soil and eliminate the need for weeding

Brunnera, geum, geranium (herbaceous *not* houseplant), iberis, nepeta and pulmonaria.

Plants with the best flowers for cutting

Coreopsis (yellow flowers); aster (blue, pink, red or violet flowers); dicentra (plum crimson, or red and white flowers); helenium (red or yellow flowers); phlox (orange, scarlet, red, purple, lilac, pink or white flowers); pyrethrum (pink, salmon or red flowers) and scabiosa (blue or white flowers).

Plants for ornamental pools

Water lilies, marsh marigolds, bog arum, arrowhead, water violet, water chestnut and water hyacinth.

Plants for rockeries and the edges of flower or shrub beds

Alyssum (chrome yellow flowers); aubrieta (blue, mauve or violet flowers); campanula (blue or mauve flowers); iberis (white flowers); saxifraga (yellow, pink, white or red flowers); sedum (yellow or rosy red flowers) and thymus (lavender, crimson, white or mauve flowers).

Once you have obtained several herbaceous plants, you can increase your stock of them by propagation. All you have to do is dig them up in either September or March, and divide them by pulling them apart with your fingers. With some plants you may need to prise them apart with a fork. You then replant the best pieces of the original plants in soil prepared as described earlier. One important thing to note is that a herbaceous border does not look at its best with border plants mingled throughout. Large clumps of one variety of plant should be planted together for an impact from their colour and character. Try not to shape the clumps too evenly but let one drift naturally into the next.

Opposite page: A well-stocked herbacious border creates an eye-catching splash of colour.
Below left: The water-lily has exotic cupped flowers; below right: capanula is easy to grow for a rockery; below: the peony needs no staking.

Bulbs

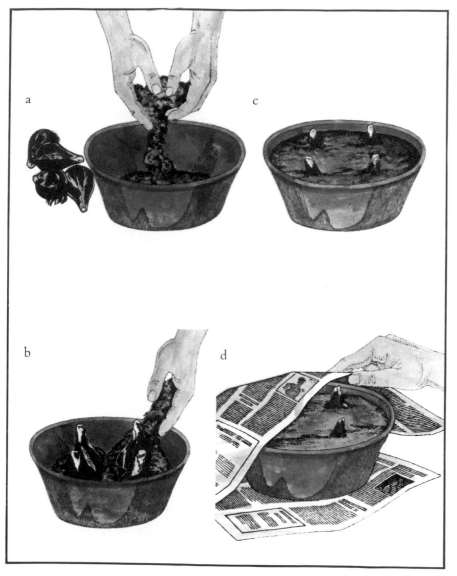

For winter indoor displays: a) put a layer of fresh bulb fibre at the base of the bowl; b) set the bulbs upright in this and cover with fibre; c) firm the fibre; d) keep the bowls in a cool dark spot until the first shoots appear.

In spring there are few greater pleasures than being able to see the brilliant colours of bulbs: snowdrops, crocuses, daffodils, tulips and hyacinths all mingling happily among shrubs and other plants.

The smaller bulbs, snowdrops, winter aconites, scillas, irises and crocuses are in fact best planted in small groups under shrubs and among the herbaceous plants, where they can be left undisturbed and allowed to multiply over the years.

The jewel colours of these little bulbs can make a dull corner sparkle. Yellow and cream daffodils and narcissus look best near the green of grass or with a background of dark conifers and hedges. Tulips can be planted in shrub or herbaceous beds and also in tubs on patios. Some of the so-called

botanical tulips are a far better choice for a small garden than the stately Darwins.

There is, for instance, the botanical tulip, *Tulipa praestans* 'Fusilier', which grows to a mere 15cm (6in) tall; yet it produces two to four orange scarlet flowers on a single stem. Look out too for some of the Greigii and hybrid tulips. Perlina at 25cm (10in) tall has heads of a lovely silvery-salmon rose colour and, as an added bonus, the leaves are blotched with chocolate brown. Yet another example of a botanical tulip is the Kaufmanniana tulip called Heart's Delight. It is 23cm (9in) tall, and the flowers are carmine-red edged with rosy white, and inside pale rose. The great advantage of these particular tulips is that unlike Cottage, Darwin, Parrot, Rembrandt, Triumph or Lily flowering kind, they do not need to be lifted after flowering. Instead they can be left safely in the ground to multiply from year to year.

When choosing daffodils and narcissus, consider too some of the smaller varieties of the cyclamineus species (for example, February Gold, Jenny, Little Witch and Peeping Tom) and also the scented Jonquils, because some of the taller daffodils are much more suited to parks than small suburban gardens.

Planting

Most spring flowering bulbs should be planted in the August and September of the previous year for best results. Tulips are the exception, and will give a better initial performance if you delay planting to the middle of November.

It is important to plant your bulbs at the correct depth. Narcissus should be planted at 15cm (6in); hyacinth, 14cm (5½in); tulip, 12cm (4½in); scilla, 10cm (4in); crocus, 8cm (3in); grape hyacinth, snowdrop and bulbs of similar size, 6cm (2in); fritillaria, winter aconite, anemone and all small bulbs, 4cm (1½in).

If you want to have bulbs in flower indoors at Christmas or early spring, you should plant them in bowls containing bulb fibre in September or October. The bowls should then be kept in a cool dark spot, such as a garage until the first shoots begin to appear. Gradually increase the amount of light the bulbs get, and eventually move them to a warm room and a sunny window ledge to flower. Crocuses, daffodils, hyacinths and tulips are the best bulbs for indoors. Many bulb firms also sell 'prepared' bulbs which have been advanced in their growth cycle so that they will flower indoors at Christmas when planted as described.

When planting bulbs, many people tend to ignore the summer kinds. Yet bulbs such as lilies are the most beautiful and powerfully scented of all. Plant your chosen varieties in October (the exception is the Madonna Lily, which should be planted in August), in soil lightened by the addition of peat. Put the bulbs in so that they lie at a depth of three times the height of the bulb, which could be 15cm (6in) deep. Madonna lilies are the exception: they should be covered with just 5cm (2in) of soil. Once planted lilies should not be disturbed. Feeding too is unnecessary. Simply give them a covering of 10cm (4in) of moist peat every spring.

Gladioli are another group of summer bulbs well worth planting from March to May 10cm to 15cm (4in to 6in) deep, in clumps or rows, and 20cm (8in) apart. The idea of planting over several months is to have a succession of flowers from July to the first frosts when the bulbs should be lifted.

Tubers

The dahlia has tuberous roots, which, because they can be lifted and planted from year to year, can also be thought of as bulbs. The tubers should be started into growth in a box of moist peat stood on a sunny window ledge in April. In late May or early June when the risk of frost has passed, they can be planted outdoors 5cm (2in) deep and between 30cm and 60cm (1ft to 2ft) apart, depending on the eventual height of the plants. Tall plants will require stout stakes. Liquid feeding and regular watering will be repaid by an increase in the number of flowers. When the stems are blackened by the first frosts, dig up the tubers, cut off most of the stems, and dry the tubers by placing them upside down in a well-ventilated place for at least a fortnight. During this period they will have lost excess moisture, and will be ready for winter storage. Store them in a box of dry peat in a frost-free place.

Another tuberous rooted plant is the begonia. The corms, or bulbs, hollow side uppermost, should be pressed into 7.5cm (3in) diameter peat pots, containing peat-based compost, in April and started into growth. The plants can be put outdoors after the risk of frost has passed, either in the open ground, or in tubs, window boxes and hanging baskets.

After the first frosts, the begonia corms should be lifted, dried and stored for the following year as in the case of gladioli and dahlias.

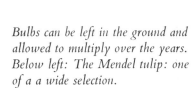

Month by month guide to flowers from bulbs

January: *Crocus ancyrensis*, winter aconites and snowdrops.

February: *Crocus biflorus*, chrysanthus varieties and sieberi varieties, *Iris reticulata* hybrids, *Narcissus cyclamineus* varieties, scillas and tulipa 'Violet Queen'.

March: *Anemone blanda* varieties, chionodoxa, *Crocus tomasinianus* varieties, Dutch crocus, grape hyacinths, narcissus varieties, *Tulipa eichleri*, praestans and varieties, and Kaufmanniana hybrids.

April: *Anemone appenina*, 'de Caen' and 'St. Brigid' varieties, dog's tooth violets, fritillaria varieties, hyacinths, narcissus varieties including jonquils, *Ornithogalum nutans*, Tulipa species, also Fosteriana hybrids and gregii hybrids, Early, Mendel, Triumph and Darwin tulips.

May: Allium, narcissus varieties, star of Bethlehem, sparaxis, tulips: Darwin, Cottage, Rembrandt, Parrot and Lily-flowered.

June: *Gladiolus nanus* varieties, lilium varieties.

July: Begonia, gladiolus: butterfly large-flowered and primulinus, lilium varieties, montbretia, chincherinchee and oxalis.

August: *Colchicum autumnale*, dahlia, freesia (outdoor) and lilium varieties.

Bulbs can be left in the ground and allowed to multiply over the years. Below left: The Mendel tulip: one of a a wide selection. Below right: The 'Caprilla' Iris has large, handsome flowers. Below: Narcissus varieties are popular for their sweet smell and brilliant colours.

Shrubs & Climbers

Above: Wisteria and clematis: climbers provide another attractive dimension in the garden. Opposite page, below left: There are many varieties of clematis blooming over a period from April to October. This variety, 'Nellie Moser' flowers profusely in early summer. Opposite page, top and bottom: Perovskia benefits from being cut hard back; this will make it throw up good flowering shoots.

The trouble with shrubs and climbers for most people is that there are so many of them. Deciding what to plant is a problem in itself. Your best course of action is to take a look around and see what grows well in your neighbourhood. You should also visit your local garden centre over several months of the year, where you will be able to examine container grown bushes with their leaves and flowers, so that you can decide on your preferences.

On a more practical note you should also consider what your garden can accommodate. Most nursery catalogues give you the eventual height of trees and shrubs. You will have to determine too whether your garden soil is acid, alkaline or neutral. You can do this quite easily with a soil test kit, or you can look for the

natural signs around you.

Alkaline soils provide the conditions in which hawthorn, beech, viburnum, lavender, escallonia, genista and lilac thrive. If there are a lot of these around, you can draw certain conclusions. Acid soils are characterised by the large number of conifers, heathers, camellias and rhododendrons growing in the area. Neutral soils give no such clear indications, and gardens generally have a mixture of all kinds of shrubs and trees.

The next question to ask yourself is how much shelter does your garden provide. Even in the same town there can be great variations in the sort of damage one can expect from the wind and frost. In the end, of course, you will simply discover by trial and error what will and will not grow –

which surely is half the fun of gardening. It is those unexpected triumphs which make all the effort worth while.

Planting

Before planting any shrub, it is essential to dig over the ground thoroughly and to enrich it when necessary with garden compost or peat. Plenty of peat added to soil which is not excessively alkaline is generally enough to tilt the balance and to allow such shrubs as rhododendrons and camellias to be grown.

It is better not to add any fertilizers to the soil at planting time. Once the shrubs have had a chance to establish themselves their roots will be in better condition to receive any food you wish to give them. The normal planting season used to be between October and March, but since most shrubs are now container grown you can plant at any time when the weather is suitable. Newly planted shrubs must however always have plenty of water and they should be supplied with supporting stakes if necessary. A moisture-retaining and weed-suppressing layer of compost placed around each shrub's roots every April is usually sufficient to keep it healthy.

Pruning

Another problem which besets the new gardener is whether or not (as well as when and how) to prune shrubs. The simple answer is that many shrubs do not need pruning at all. None of the evergreens do, except where a particular shrub has become overgrown. Then it is simply a case of giving it a quick trim after flowering. Many of the slower growing deciduous shrubs need no pruning either – for example, azaleas, corylopsis, *Daphne mezereum*, *Hibiscus syriacus*, *Hamamelis mollis*, most hydrangeas, lilacs, *Magnolia stellata* and *Viburnum fragrans*.

The shrubs (and climbers) which do

need pruning are the fast unruly growers. These can, for convenience, be placed in two main groups. Those which flower in spring and early summer on shoots which they produced the previous year, and secondly those which flower after July and in autumn on shoots grown during the current year.

Typical examples of group one are forsythia, *Clematis montana*, flowering currant, deutzias, kerria, philadelphus and weigela. These can all be pruned immediately after flowering by cutting away those shoots which have just flowered. Such shoots can be recognised because they usually are a darker colour than the new ones.

Typical examples of group two are *Buddleia davidii*, caryopteris, deciduous ceonothus, hypericum 'Hidcote', fuchsia, perovskia, spiraea, and tamarix.

The aim with these particular shrubs is to encourage them to make plenty of young shoots which in turn will bear flowers. Pruning is normally carried out in April, or immediately before growth starts in spring. Cut back each shoot to about 2.5cm (1in) of the base of the previous season's growth. In the case of perovskia, caryopteris, fuchsia and Spiraea Anthony Waterer this may mean cutting the shrubs back to ground level. If with some of the other shrubs, you wish to retain a number of branches for screening purposes, it is sufficient to cut all shoots by half their length.

Choosing shrubs

What shrubs should you grow? The chart shows a selection growing no more than 1 metre (3ft) tall which are ideal for today's small gardens. Below are some suggestions for special situations.

Chalky soil: berberis, buddleia, chaenomeles, choisya, cistus, clematis, cornus, cotoneaster, daphne, deutzia, diervilla, escallonia, euonymus, forsythia, hibiscus, hypericum, holly, lilac, philadelphus, potentilla, ribes, senecio, spiraea, viburnum.

Sunless positions: azalea, berberis, camellia, daphne, euonymus, gaultheria, hypericum, mahonia, olearia, pachysandra, pernettya, ribes, sarcococca, skimmia, vinca.

Many shrubs, as well as being grown in beds in the garden, can also be grown against walls. In certain gardens, exposed to wind and frost, this may be the only way in which some shrubs can be grown. Prior to planting it is essential to remove the soil

Above: The hypericum will flourish on chalky soil.

to about two spades' depths and to enrich the soil with plenty of compost or moist peat before returning it to the planting hole. Here is a selection of shrubs for walls: use it as a guide to help choose a satisfactory rotation which can ensure blooms and fragrance all year round.

Against walls: camellia (N or W); ceanothus (S or W); chaenomeles (any aspect); chimonanthus (S or W); choisya (S or W); *Cotoneaster horizontalis* (any aspect); escallonia (S or W); garrya (any aspect); kerria (any aspect); *Magnolia grandiflora* (S or W); *Prunus triloba* (S or W); pyracantha (any aspect), *Viburnum burkwoodii* (any aspect).

Such shrubs can be trained against wood, or plastic trellis fixed to the wall or you can simply put up some horizontal wires secured to pieces of ironmongery called 'vine eyes' fixed to the wall. With the plants and shrubs normally regarded as 'climbers', such support is vital. The chart shows some suitable climbers with their preffered aspects, the height to which they can be expected to grow, and also their particular attraction whether it is bright flowers, fragrance or attractive leaves.

Shrub	Months of Interest	Scent
Jap azaleas (E)	May and June	No
Cistus crispus (E)	May to July	No
Caryopteris		
Clandonensis	September and October	No
Cystissus beanii	May	Faint
Cystissus kewensis	April to May	Faint
Daphne cneorum	April to May	Yes
Erica carnea vars (E)	November to April	No
Erica darleyensis (E)	January to April	No
Erica cinerea (E)	June to August	No
Erica tetralix (E)	June to October	No
Erica vagans (E)	July to September	No
Calluna varieties (E)	July to October	No
Forsythia tetragold	February to March	No
Fuchsia Tom Thumb	August to October	No
Gaultheria procumbens (E)	July flowers, berries autumn, winter	No
Genista Lydia	May and June	Faint
Hebe in variety (E)	June to September	No
Hydrangea preziosa	August and September	No
Helichrysum splendidum (E)	August and September	No
Hypericum moserianum	July and August	Faint
Lavendula in variety (E)	July and August	V. fragrant
Mahonia aquifolium (E)	March to May	Yes
Olearia haastii (E)	July and August	No
Osmanthus delavayi	April	Yes
Pachysandra terminalis (E)	March	No
Pernettya hybrids (E)	All winter	No
Perovskia Blue Spire	August and September	No
Philadelphus		
Manteau d'Hermine	June	Yes
Phlomis fruticosa (E)	June and July	No
Potentilla in variety	May to October	No
Rhododendron dwarf hybrids (E)	April to May	No
Salvia lavandulifolia	June	Yes
Sarcococca humilis (E)	January and February	Yes
Stephanandra incisa crispa (E)	March to May	No
Vinca in variety (E)	March to May	No

Key
E = Evergreen

Climber	Height	Aspect	Scent	Attraction
Actinidia chinensis	6m (20ft)	S or W	Yes	Flowers and fruit
Actinidia kolomikta	4m (12ft)	S or W	No	Leaves pink, white
Akebia quinata	6m (20ft)	S or W	Yes	Flowers and fruit
Aristolochia macrophylla	6m (20ft)	Any	No	Flowers, lovely leaves
Campsis radicans 'Madame Galen'	5m (16ft)	S or W	No	Flowers
Clematis montana in variety	6m (20ft)	N or any	No	Flowers
Clematis hybrids	3m to 5m (10ft to 16ft)	Any	No	Flowers
Hedera helix in variety (E)	6m (20ft)	Any	No	Leaves
Jasminum nudiflorum	4m (13ft)	Any	Yes	Flowers
Jasminum officinale	8m (26ft)	E, S, or W	Yes	Scent
Lonicera henryi (E)	4m (13ft)	E or W	No	Leaves, flowers
Lonicera japonica Halliana (E)	5m (16ft)	Any	Yes	Leaves, flowers
Lonicera periclymenum 'Serotina'	5m (16ft)	N, E, or W	Yes	Flowers
Passiflora caerulea (E)	8m (26ft)	S or W	Yes	Flowers, fruits
Polygonum baldschuanicum	12m (40ft)	Any	No	Covering power
Parthenocissus quinquefolia (Virginia Creeper)	12m (40ft)	Any	No	Brilliant foliage
Wisteria floribunda	4m (13ft)	S or W	Yes	Flowers, scent
Wisteria sinensis	12m (40ft)	S or W	Yes	Flowers, scent

Key
E = Evergreen

Roses

Just as no garden would be complete without a climber or two on the house walls, some people might argue that it would not be a garden in the first place without some roses, which are surely the most popular of all shrubs.

The choice of roses is almost bafflingly large. However, roses can be split into two basic groups. First there are the tea roses, so-called because when they were first introduced their scent reminded people of newly opened tea chests. These particular roses are still the best choice for perfume and quality flowers. The second group of roses includes those called floribundas because of the number of flowers produced at one time on a single bush. If it is mainly colour you are after, these are by far the best choice. Roses can be planted in beds by themselves or in small groups as part of a herbaceous or shrub border.

Planting

The best time for planting is between November and March during mild wea-

Left above: The hybrid tea rose 'Ernest Morse' has a rich fragrance.
Left: Floribunda rose 'Arthur Bell'.

ther when the soil is workable. Roses bought in containers can be planted at any time of the year.

If roses arrive from the nursery when the weather is unsuitable for planting, unpack them in a shed or garage but keep the roots covered. Then before you can plant, soak the roots in water for several hours. The soil for roses should be thoroughly prepared and improved if necessary with compost. When planting a rose bush, dig a hole with a spade, place the bush in with its roots spread and fill the hole with a mixture of soil and damp peat so that the bulge on the rootstock, where the rose was grafted, is at or a little below soil level.

Bush roses should be 38cm to 45cm (15in to 18in) apart, depending on their eventual height. Standard roses should be 90cm to 180cm (3ft to 6ft) apart. Newly planted roses need no feeding the first year, but they do require pruning. In February or March all weak, dead, or frost-damaged shoots should be cut cleanly away at an outward facing bud on bush and standard roses. The remaining branches should be cut back to three or five buds; the sturdier shoots are not cut back as hard as the less vigorous ones. In future years the same pruning principles apply, except that floribunda roses need not be cut back so severely.

Those old-fashioned roses called shrub, species and modern shrub need hardly any pruning at all apart from the occasional thinning out and the removal of dead wood. Climbing roses too should not be pruned any more than is necessary, but merely thinned out and confined to their own particular area of the garden.

Care

Roses should be fed with a proprietary granular rose fertilizer in April, June and July as directed by the manufacturers. Routine spraying with a systemic fungicide between April and September will give protection to those roses susceptible to mildew and blackspot. Aphids are best dealt with by spraying with a suitable insecticide when they are first noticed. In April too you can put down a 5cm (2in) thick moisture-retaining and weed-suppressing layer of moist peat around the bushes.

Bush roses are available in several heights from 38cm to 120cm (15in to 4ft) tall. For convenience we can classify them as tall, medium or low growing.

Types of roses

Tea roses: Alec's Red (cherry red, fragrant, medium); Alexander (vermilion, tall); Blessings (pink, fragrant, medium); Diorama (apricot, fragrant, medium); Ena Harkness (scarlet, fragrant, medium); Ernest H. Morse (red, fragrant, tall); Fragrant Cloud (orange-red, fragrant, medium); Mischief (salmon, fragrant, medium); Mullard Jubilee (pink, fragrant, medium); Pascali (white, tall); Perfecta (cream, fragrant, tall); Whisky Mac (gold, fragrant, medium).

Floribundas: Allgold (yellow, low); Anne Crocker (red, tall); Arthur Bell (yellow, fragrant, tall); Evelyn Fison (orange scarlet, medium); Iceberg (white, tall); Lilli Marlene (scarlet, medium); Living Fire (orange and scarlet, medium); Orange Sensation (fragrant, medium); Pineapple Poll (orange yellow, fragrant, low); Queen Elizabeth (pink, very tall); Tip Top (salmon, fragrant, low); Topsi (orange scarlet, low).

Many standard roses are also obtainable in these particular varieties. Similarly there are climbing versions too of some of these varieties.

Climbers: Bantry Bay (pink, vigorous, healthy foliage); Danse du Feu (orange-scarlet, very vigorous, good for north wall); Golden Showers (yellow, fragrant, moderate growth, very free flowering); Handel (cream and pink, vigorous, bronze-tinted foliage); New Dawn (pink, very fragrant, moderate growth, free flowering); Schoolgirl (apricot, fragrant, vigorous); Swan Lake (white, vigorous, constantly in flower).

Below: A climbing rose is ideal for a pergola or trellis. Opposite page: The cones of the Norway spruce are attractive in their shape and smoothness.

Trees

Now that we have added colour to our gardens with plants, bulbs, shrubs and roses, there is just one thing missing – a tree. Choosing trees can make or mar a garden. It is vital to get trees with both the right shape and eventual size to fit in with their surroundings. Use the chart to help you to decide what is most suitable for you. It is also worth remembering, incidentally, that with a small garden some of the larger shrubs, can be regarded as trees.

The problem with most trees is that they lose their leaves in autumn and leave the garden looking rather bleak over the winter and early spring. The solution is to have some conifers in the garden to add a little colour and interest when such assistance is most needed. The charts give lists of conifers which would suit small to medium-sized gardens, and smaller ones which would fill the odd gap or smother an unsightly object such as a manhole cover.

Trees and conifers all need the same soil preparation as shrubs. However, in many cases it will also be necessary to provide a stout stake for support and a proper 'tree-tie' for security, until such time as the trees are capable of standing on their own. Remember too, if planting on grass to leave a weed-free circle of soil at least 90cm (3ft) in diameter, so that the trees can obtain sufficient moisture.

Some of the conifers are small growing and are useful for a rock-garden or for planting on banks. Others have interesting and attractive cones which can be used for house-hold decorations especially on festive occasions. Some conifers have a particularly attractive appearance due to their marked colouring, including the Picea pungens glauca which has lovely blue-green branches.

Name	Size after 10 years	Attraction	Soil
Almond			
Prunus dulcis	H. 3.60m S. 1.5m (12ft by 5ft)	Pink flowers in March	Any
Birch			
Betula pendula	H.5.60cm S.2.40cm (18ft by 8ft)	Silvery white bark	Any
Japanese Cherry			
Prunus erecta	H. 3m S. 60cm (10ft by 2ft)	Pink flowers in April (slim growth)	Any
Prunus Pink perfection	H. 3.60m S. 2.10m (12ft by 7ft)	Pink flowers in April	Any
Weeping Cherry			
Prunus Kiku-shidare Sakura	H. 3m S. 2.10m (10ft by 7ft)	Pink flowers March/April (slow growing)	Any
Crab apple			
Malus floribunda	H. 3.60m S. 3m (12ft by 10ft)	Pink flowers April/May	Any
Malus coronaria 'Charlottae'	H. 4.20m S. 2.10m (14ft by 7ft)	Scented pink flowers May and June	Any
False acacia			
Robina frisia	H. 4.50m S. 2.40m (15ft by 8ft)	Golden yellow leaves	Any
Holly			
Ilex aquifolium J.C. van Tol	H. 3m S. 1.80m (10ft by 6ft)	Smooth green leaves, red berries, self fertile	Any
Paperbark maple			
Acer griseum	H. 3.60m S. 1.80m (12ft by 6ft)	Red leaves in Autumn, bark peels to show cinnamon colour	Any
Mountain Ash (Rowan)			
Sorbus Joseph Rock	H. 4.20m S. 2.10m (14ft by 7ft)	Autumnal leaves of orange, red, purple, yellow berries	Neutral or acid
Weeping Willow			
Salix purpurea pendula	H. 3.60m S. 2.70m (12ft by 9ft)	Catkins, bluish green leaves, purplish twigs.	Any, provided moist

Key   H = Height   S = Spread

Far right: Chamaecyparis lawsoniana 'Stewartii' has golen-tipped foliage.
Right: A narrow form of spruce, suitable for a small garden is Picea omorika.

Conifers for small to medium size gardens

Name	Size after 10 years	Foliage	Soil
Cupressus macrocarpa 'Donard Gold'	H. 3m S. 90cm (10ft by 3ft)	Golden yellow	Any
Juniperus communis 'Hibernica'	H. 2.40m S. 60cm (8ft by 24in)	Silvery green	Any
Juniperus virginiana 'Skyrocket'	H. 2.10m S. 38cm (7ft by 15in)	Blue grey	Any
Lawson's cypress			
Chamaecyparis lawsoniana columnaris	H. 3m S. 60cm (10ft by 24in)	Blue green	Any
'Ellwoodii'	H. 1.80m S. 90cm (6ft by 3ft)	Blue green	Any
'Penbury Blue'	H. 2.40m S. 60cm (8ft by 24in)	Silver blue	Any
'Stewartii'	H. 2.40m S. 1.20m (8ft by 4ft)	Yellowish green	Any
Mountain Pine			
Pinus mugo	H. 90cm S. 1.50m (3ft by 5ft)	Bright green	Any but, best on lime
Spruce			
Picea pungens glauca 'Koster'	H. 1.80m S. 60cm (6ft by 24in)	Silver blue	Moist, acid or neutral

Small conifers

Name	Size after 10 years	Foliage	Soil
Juniperus communis compressa	H. 3.8cm S 15cm (15in by 6in)	Bluish grey	Any
Hornibrookii	H. 15cm S. 1.20m (6in by 4ft)	Green and bronze	Any
J.Horizontalis	H. 7.5cm S. 90cm (3in by 3ft)	Grey green	Any
'Bar Harbor'			
Lawson's cypress			
Chamaecyparis lawsoniana minima aurea	H. 38cm S. 25cm (15in by 10in)	Gold	Any
Pisifera 'Boulevard'	H. 1.20m S. 60mc (4ft by 24in)	Silver blue	Lime free
Mountain pine			
Pinus mugo 'Mops'	H. 38cm S. 60cm (15in by 24in)	Bright green, creamy shoots	Any, but good on lime
Spruce			
Picea glauca albertiana	H. 60cm S. 25cm (24in by 10in)	Bright green	Any
Western Red Cedar			
Thuja occidentalis 'Rheingold'	H. 1.20m S. 90cm (4ft by 3ft)	Bronze and gold	Any

Key
H = Height
S = Spread

FOOD FOR THOUGHT

Understanding your soil and preparing the ground carefully can result in the great satisfaction of providing your family's vegetables from your own garden.

Vegetables

Above: Fresh garden vegetables as a source of vitamins are unrivalled. The gardener who can grow sound produce as shown here will be saving money and promoting good health within the family.

Even with the smallest of gardens you should grow some vegetables. Not just for the money you will save, but for the sheer satisfaction of providing some of your own food.

Preparing the soil

The first step to growing your own vegetables is to prepare the soil adequately, for your ultimate success will stand or fall by how well you do this basic task. The time for digging is in late autumn or early winter if you want to be able to sow in the spring. As a general rule, the heavier your soil the longer it requires to be weathered by winter rain and frost before it is sufficiently friable to make a bed for sowing seed.

The second step is to make the soil suitable for particular vegetables, because there are three basic groups of vegetables with different requirements. There are the root crops such as beetroot, carrot, parsnip, potato, swede and turnip which require the addition of a general vegetable fertilizer to the soil before sowing. Next, there are the brassicas: vegetables such as broccoli, Brussels sprouts, cabbage, cauliflower and spinach. The soil for these vegetables should be limed if necessary in winter – make a soil test (see page 10) – and give a top dressing of general fertilizer before sowing or plant-

ing. Thirdly, there are all the other crops such as beans, celery, cucumber, endive, leek, lettuce, marrow, onion, peas, radish, sweet corn and tomato. The soil for these vegetables should be enriched with compost when you do your autumn or winter digging and top dressed with general fertilizer before sowing or planting.

Crop rotation and timing

The three groups of vegetables provide the reason, as well as the necessity, for practising some form of crop rotation so that the soil has a chance to recover from the demands placed upon it. Another good reason for rotating your crops is that it helps to prevent disease. In really small plots proper rotation may not be possible, but by careful planning you should be able to avoid growing the same vegetable from a particular group in the same position two years running.

The third step to success is to sow and plant out at the correct time. No matter what it says on the seed packet or in the books, only you can determine your local conditions. For instance, if the weather is cold and wet in spring, wait a little. You will gain nothing by attempting to sow in unsuitable conditions, and when sowing, make allowances for the quality of your soil. A depth of 2.5cm (1in) may be fine in light soil, but on heavy ground 1cm ($\frac{1}{2}$in) will be safer if you want the seeds to germinate. You can also help by sowing the seeds thinly so that they are not competing for moisture, light and air.

Maximum productivity

The fourth step is to get the maximum productivity out of your plot by a technique called intercropping. Some vegetables mature in weeks while others take months before they are ready for harvesting. So you can grow fast-maturing crops between rows of the slower-maturing vegetables. Between rows of beans (broad, French and runner) you can grow lettuces, radishes and beetroots. Broad beans can also be inter-cropped with Brussels sprouts. The brassicas themselves can be intercropped with lettuce, beetroots and dwarf beans; and between the rows of celery you can have dwarf beans, peas and lettuces.

Another example of getting maximum productivity is called catch-cropping. This is the practice of growing a fast-maturing crop in ground that is empty for only a short period between the harvesting of one crop and the sowing and planting of another. An example of this system is the sowing of carrots (in early spring) on ground which will later be planted with cabbages (in early summer). Radishes are a good catch crop as they mature in six or seven weeks from sowing. Accurate timing is vital as if you sow your catch crop too late, it will not have matured in time for you to plant the main crop.

Not all seeds can be sown directly out of doors. Some such as celery and tomatoes have to be sown indoors and planted out-doors once the risk of frost has passed. Some vegetable plants too can be raised by sowing the seeds directly into peat pots or peat blocks. This practice is most useful with brassicas and produces better yields in areas with poor growing conditions.

Growing vegetables in towns

Growing vegetables is something which people who live in the country take for granted. For them it is often the main activity in the garden. However, what about the millions of people who live in towns and cities and who through sheer pressure of space can never grow all the vegetables which they would like?

The solution calls for a little ingenuity. It is amazing what can be achieved on a small patio garden, or a sunny balcony for that matter, by growing vegetables in window boxes, tubs, plastic sacks of compost, called 'growing bags', and ordinary plastic pots.

Window boxes are good for salad crops such as spring onions, radishes, beetroot and lettuce. In fact the lettuce varieties Tom Thumb, Little Gem, and Winter Density might well have been produced specially for window boxes: they are so small and compact, and, in-cidentally, just perfect for a salad for two.

Tubs can provide a home for dwarf French beans, carrots and all the salad crops covered in this chapter. If you put some canes into the tub and tie them to-gether at the top to form the shape of a Red Indian tepee, you can also grow some runner beans.

Growing bags are the ideal containers for cucumbers, bush tomatoes and courg-ettes. Plastic pots, stood in sunny corners, can contain aubergines and capsicums. You could also grow potatoes in 30cm (12in) diameter plastic pots by half-filling the pots with compost, planting one tuber in each, and topping up the pots with compost whenever green leaves break the surface of the compost.

For crops such as lettuce the containers could be filled with good loam, purchased from a garden centre, but for the other vegetables you will be better with John Innes No. 3 compost or one of the peat-based composts.

Below: There are numerous kinds of vegetable to choose from, and varieties to suit every type of garden. Maximum productivity will be achieved by careful planning and preparation within the scope of the land available no matter how limited this is.

Brassicas

A well-formed head of cabbage. It is not difficult to produce a succession of these useful vegetables throughout the year.

several months in advance of planting. The seed should be sown thinly in rows 1.3cm ($\frac{1}{2}$in) deep. Winter varieties: sow outdoors at the end of April or May and transplant during June; spring varieties: sow in July and August and transplant in September or October; summer varieties: sow indoors or under glass in February and plant out at the beginning of April. You can also sow outdoors in April and transplant in May or June. The seedlings should be transplanted to their final positions when they have six leaves. About two weeks previously give the plot a dressing of 112g/m² (4oz to the sq yd) of vegetable fertilizer. When transplanting, firm the soil around the plants and water thoroughly. Allow 30cm to 45cm (12in to 18in) between the plants each way depending on the variety. Hoe the soil lightly to keep down weeds and water regularly as a sudden drought ruins the flavour of cabbages.

Pests and diseases
Aphids, caterpillars, club root and root fly.

Harvesting
Cut fresh from the garden as required.

Brussels Sprouts
Sowing to harvest time: 28 to 36 weeks depending on the variety.
Yield: 1kg (2lb) of sprouts to a plant.
Soil type: Firm soil rich in humus.

Brussels sprouts are a splendid green crop for winter months when little else may be available. As with cabbages grow the modern small hybrid varieties which are ideal for the average garden.

Sowing and planting
The soil for Brussels sprouts should be prepared in the same way as for cabbages. The seed should be sown thinly outdoors between March and April, depending on the variety and location, 1.3cm ($\frac{1}{2}$in) deep. When the seedlings are 15cm (6in) high, they are ready to be transplanted to their permanent positions. But first firm the soil with your feet, give it a dressing of 112g/m² (4oz to a square yd) of vegetable fertilizer and rake it level. When transplanting, set the plants in holes 60cm (24in) apart each way which have previously been filled with water, unless the soil is already

Cabbage: winter/spring or summer
Sowing to harvest time: Summer and winter varieties 20 to 35 weeks; spring varieties 25 weeks.
Yield: 1kg to 2kg (2lb to 4lb) a plant.
Soil type: Ordinary well-drained garden soil, well-consolidated and free from air pockets.

Cabbages grow well even in areas where weather conditions are generally poor. Make use of the modern smaller varieties so that maximum benefit from the available space can be obtained.

Sowing and planting
As cabbages require well-consolidated soil, preparation of the plot should be carried out

moist. The lowest pair of leaves on each plant should touch the soil, which should be firmed with your fingers. Hoe the soil regularly and water well in dry spells. Seedlings need protection from sparrows, while the mature crop is a favourite with pigeons. In windy areas draw soil up the stems or tie the stems to bamboo canes in the autumn.

Pests and diseases

Aphids, birds, caterpillars, club root, flea beetles and root fly.

Harvesting

Start to pick the sprouts at the bottom of the stem and when they are still tightly closed. This will encourage the sprouts further up the stem to mature. Do not remove the tops until the end of the winter as they give protection during severe weather. Store by freezing.

Cauliflower

Sowing to harvest time: 18 to 24 weeks for summer and autumn.
Varieties: 40 weeks for winter varieties.
Yield: 1kg (2lb) per plant.
Soil type: Rich loam, but sandy soils are suitable if plenty of organic material is dug in during winter.

Summer cauliflowers are in season from July to September; autumn varieties from October to December and winter cauliflowers from January to March.

Sowing and planting

All varieties require soil well prepared by digging in plenty of compost and limed if necessary. Just before transplanting give the soil a dressing of 112g/m² (4oz to the sq yd) of vegetable fertilizer. Summer varieties should be sown indoors in January and set outside in April to provide a July crop.

Autumn cauliflowers should be sown outdoors in April and May and transplanted in late June. Winter varieties should be sown outdoors in May and transplanted in July. The seed outdoors should be sown 1.3cm (½in) deep. The seedlings are ready to transplant when they have six leaves. Set the plants in holes which have previously been filled with water, if the soil is not already moist, 60cm (24in) apart at the same level as they were on the seed bed. Cauliflowers must be kept well watered. If they wilt, they are unlikely later to produce firm tight heads. A light dressing of 28g (1oz) of nitrate of soda or nitro chalk given to each plant twice during its growing season improves the quality and quantity of the curds. Summer varieties should have a few leaves bent over the curds to protect them from the sun. With winter varieties a similar measure protects the curds from frost and snow.

Pests and diseases

Aphids, caterpillars, club root, flea beetle and root fly.

Harvesting

Cut cauliflowers while they are still small and tender. Summer and autumn varieties are at their best if cut in the morning with dew still on the curds. In frosty weather winter cauliflowers are best cut at midday. Cauliflowers hung upside down in a shed remain in good condition for two weeks. Otherwise, store by freezing.

Above: Brussels sprouts are popular not only because picking can be extended over a long period but also because they can stand up to severe winter weather.

Below: The cauliflower will produce a rewarding result if it is grown on deeply dug soil with plenty of organic matter.

Above top: Purple sprouting broccoli is one of the most delicious members of the cabbage family.
Above: White sprouting broccoli is a prolific cropper.
Opposite page, bottom: Spinach beet successfully fills a gap at the end of the winter when other vegetables are scarce. It can withstand frost and will continue producing a constant supply of greens throughout the winter.
Opposite page, centre: New Zealand spinach can survive very hot and dry conditions.
Opposite page, top: Spinach is a nutritious vegetable for summer and autumn.

Broccoli: calabrese, purple and white

Sowing to harvest time: 12 weeks for calabrese; 40 weeks for purple and white varieties.
Yield: 1kg (2lb) per plant.
Soil type: Heavy, firm and rich in organic matter.

Broccoli is closely related to the cauliflower, but it is much easier to grow. It can withstand more heat and more cold in fact than the cabbage.

Sowing and planting

Broccoli requires soil which has been well prepared as for cabbages and which has also been firmed with your feet before planting. The seed should be sown thinly in rows 1.3cm ($\frac{1}{2}$in) deep. For calabrese (green sprouting broccoli): sow in April or May and thin early to prevent the plants from being weakened through their being overcrowded. When the seedlings are 7.5cm (3in) high, move them to their permanent positions with 46cm (18in) between the plants and 60cm (24in) between the rows. Before setting the plants in their final positions give the plot a dressing of 112g/m² (4oz to the sq yd) of vegetable fertilizer. When transplanting, fill the planting holes with water. Allow to drain. Then set the plants 2.5cm (1in) deeper in the holes than they were in the seed bed. Finally firm the soil around the plants with your fingers.

Purple sprouting broccoli is the hardiest of the sprouting broccolis and it grows well in cold areas and on heavy clay soils. Sow the seeds as before in May and transplant when the seedlings are 7.5cm (3in) high to produce a crop from December to May, depending on the variety. White sprouting broccoli sown at the same time will produce its crop from March to May, depending on the variety. All broccoli requires regular hoeing to keep down weeds and water in dry spells. Feed with 29g/m² (1oz to a sq yd) in rings around each plant with nitro chalk four weeks after transplanting. With purple and white sprouting broccoli, draw up soil around the stems in autumn, to prevent their being felled by winter winds. Alternatively provide each plant with a bamboo stake.

Pests and diseases

Birds (particularly pigeons), aphids, caterpillars, club root and root fly.

Harvesting

The time to cut is when the 'spears' are small and not too far developed, a point just before the small flower buds have opened. Cut the main centre spear first and then all the side spears. Keep cutting and never let the plant flower or production of fresh spears will stop. Store by freezing.

Spinach

Sowing to harvest time: 8 to 15 weeks.
Yield: 230g (8oz) per plant.
Soil type: Deep, moist and rich in organic matter.

Spinach is not as easy to cultivate as some other vegetables. The problem is that it has a natural tendency to run to seed instead of producing leaves. However, there are certain ways of ensuring success.

Sowing and planting

The soil for spinach should contain plenty of organic matter and be limed if necessary. Just before sowing, give the soil a dressing of 112g/m² (4oz to a sq yd) of vegetable fertilizer. Ideally summer spinach should be grown in the light shade of other taller vegetables, for instance as a catch crop between two rows of peas and beans. Sow the seeds every few weeks from March to mid-July in rows 2.5cm (1in) deep and 30cm (12in) apart. Thin the seedlings first to 7.5cm (3in) apart. Then some weeks later thin again to 15cm (6in) apart and retain the surplus plants for eating. Winter spinach should be sown in August, or September (in warm areas), for harvesting between October and April. In cold districts cover the crop with cloches in late autumn to protect it from frost. Hoe the soil around the plants regularly to keep down weeds and to prevent its forming a crust. Plenty of water is vital during dry spells.

Pests and diseases

Aphids, damping off.

Harvesting

Cut away the outer leaves of plants with scissors as soon as they have reached an acceptable size. Continual picking will encourage fresh growth. With summer varieties up to half the leaves can be removed at a picking. With winter varieties, remove only a quarter of the leaves at any one time. Store by freezing.

New Zealand Spinach

Sowing to harvest time: 8 to 10 weeks.

Yield: 1kg (2lb) per plant, but the more you pick the more the plant will produce.

Soil type: Deep, moist and rich in organic matter.

New Zealand 'Spinach' is not really a spinach, but it is a very good substitute where the summers are often too dry for successful spinach growing. Though tolerant of droughts, the leaves will be more succulent if watered regularly.

The soil should be prepared as for ordinary spinach. In mid-May the seeds should be soaked in water overnight to soften them and so speed germination. Then they should be sown in clusters of three in rows 1.3cm ($\frac{1}{2}$in) deep with 60cm (2ft) between subsequent clusters and other rows. Later thin to leave just one plant 60cm (2ft) apart. Hoe to keep down weeds and water if necessary. When the plants measure 30cm (1ft) across, remove the growing points to encourage the formation of more young leaves.

Pests and diseases

None of any consequence.

Harvesting

Cut a few leaves regularly from each plant to encourage continued production of fresh young leaves.

Spinach beet (perpetual spinach)

Sowing to harvesting time: 8 to 14 weeks.

Yield: $\frac{1}{2}$kg (1lb) per plant, but the more you pick the more you get.

Soil type: Deep, moist and rich in organic matter, but unlike ordinary spinach will tolerate poor or sandy soil.

Spinach beet does not bolt in summer or die of cold in winter. Its mild taste is often found more acceptable by children.

real point of spinach beet is to have spinach in winter and spring when the ordinary kind is scarce. Although the beets would continue cropping for a couple of years or so, a fresh crop is best raised annually.

Silver or Seakale Beet (Swiss Chard)
Planting to harvest time: 12 weeks.
Yield: 1½kg (3lb) a plant, but the more you harvest the more you get.
Soil type: Moist with added organic matter, but will also grow in light sandy soil and heavy clay.

Seakale beet is simple to grow and it provides a supply of spinach-like greens throughout the summer and autumn.

Sowing and planting
The soil is prepared as for ordinary spinach. In April sow three seeds together 1.3cm (½in) deep every 38cm (15in) in drills 45cm (18in) apart. As soon as the seedlings can be handled easily, thin to leave the strongest one every 38cm (15in) apart. The aftercare of seakale beet is as spinach.

Pests and diseases
Virtually trouble free.

Harvesting
It is essential to remove the stems from the outside of each plant to enable the central stems to develop. The stems should be pulled like rhubarb, as cutting makes them bleed. If the beets can be covered with cloches over the winter, there will be a fresh crop of leaves for the following spring, summer and autumn. Otherwise, you will have to sow again in April.

Above: Silver or seakale beet (Swiss chard) is a hardy vegetable with a dual-purpose for cooking: the leaves are cooked like ordinary spinach and the mid-ribs like asparagus. Alternatively the two can be cooked together.

Sowing and planting
The soil should be prepared as for ordinary spinach. In April sow the seeds in 2.5cm (1in) deep drills, 45cm (18in) apart. Later thin the seedlings down to 20cm (8in) apart.

Pests and diseases
Virtually trouble-free.

Harvesting
The first leaves can be removed from the outside of the plants in summer. But the

Seeds & Pods

Broad Bean
Planting to harvest time: 16 weeks for spring sowings; 28 weeks for autumn sowings.
Yield: 5kg (11lb) to a 3m (10ft) double row. Dwarf varieties 2kg (4½lb) to a single row.
Soil: Ordinary, but well drained.

Broad beans are one of the easiest vegetables to grow and there are three main types. The Longpod varieties, recognised by their long, narrow pods. They are the best choice for hardiness, top yields and early crops. The Windsor varieties, distinguished by their shorter, wider pods.

Opposite page, top: French beans are at their best if picked when young and tender.
Opposite page, bottom: The broad bean is amongst the hardiest of bean crops.

These are the best choice for flavour and later crops, but they cannot be sown in autumn. The Dwarf varieties, which have short pods and dwarf bushy growth are ideal for small gardens. They are normally grown in single rows.

Sowing and planting
The soil should be well dug and enriched with compost. About a week before sowing give the soil a dressing of 112g/m² (4oz to a sq yd) of vegetable fertilizer. In mild areas the long pod varieties can be sown in November 5cm (2in) deep with 15cm (6in) between the seeds. A second

row should be sown just 23cm (9in) away. Subsequent sets of 'double rows' should be 60cm (24in) away. If possible cover with cloches over winter. All varieties can also be sown in March and April. Keep the plants well supplied with water and free from weeds.

Pests and diseases

Aphids (particularly blackfly), botrytis (grey mould), and slugs.

Harvesting

Pick the pods while the scar on each bean in the shell is green or white (not black) for top flavour. Store by freezing.

French bean
(kidney and string beans)

Planting to harvest time: 10 to 14 weeks.
Yield: 3kg ($6\frac{1}{2}$lb) to 3m (10ft) row, dwarf varieties; $4\frac{1}{2}$kg (10lb) to a 3m (10ft) row, climbing varieties.
Soil: Light and well drained.
French beans are at their best if they are picked when really small, and this is just one of the advantages of growing your own.

Sowing and planting

The soil should be enriched with compost in winter, and about a week before sowing given a dressing of 112g/m² (4oz to the sq yd) of vegetable fertilizer, which should be raked in. If you have cloches, you can begin by sowing in April in rows 5cm (2in) deep and 60cm (24in) apart. The seeds should be spaced 7.5cm (3in) apart and later thinned to 15cm (6in) apart. Without cloches you can make successional sowings from May to early June. Again if cloches are available, a sowing can be made in July to provide a late autumn crop. The cloches will be required to cover the beans in October. Climbing varieties will need the support of plastic bean netting or sticks. The soil should be hoed regularly to keep it free from weeds and well broken up. Water well in dry spells and spray the flowers gently with water in the evening to encourage pods to form.

Pests and diseases

Aphids, capsid, botrytis and slugs (particular problem with seedlings).

Harvesting

The pods are ready for picking at about 10cm (4in) long when they snap easily if bent. Do not wait until the bulges of beans are visible in the pods. Harvest several times a week if necessary so that the plants will continue to crop for six to eight weeks. Store by freezing.

Runner bean

Planting to harvest time: 12 to 16 weeks.
Yield: 18kg (40lb) to 3m (10ft) row, climbing varieties; 8kg ($17\frac{1}{2}$lb) to a 3m (10ft) row, dwarf varieties.
Soil: Moist with plenty of added compost. Heavy clay and sandy soils are unsuitable.

Runner beans are possibly the best performing crop. They are also one of the most attractive with their scarlet pink or white flowers among the lush green leaves. The most common varieties are the stick or pole runner beans, which can produce pods up to 50cm (20in) long. However, there are also dwarf runner beans with pods just 20cm (8in) long which are most suitable in small gardens or in cold, windy situations.

Sowing and planting

The soil for runner beans should be prepared in winter by digging over an area 45cm (18in) wide and the depth of the spade and incorporating a thick layer of compost in the bottom. In mild areas the seeds can be sown outdoors at the end of May, 5cm (2in) deep and 23cm (9in) apart with 38cm (15in) between the first and second row. At each 23cm (9in) interval two seeds should be placed to allow for losses and the weaker seedlings remaining should be removed soon after germination. Subsequent double rows of beans should be 1.50m (5ft) away.

In cold districts it is best to sow the seeds indoors or in a cold frame or greenhouse in early May. Sow the seeds individually in peat pots containing peat-based compost and do not plant outdoors until the roots are growing strongly through the sides of the pots. Climbing beans will require support from poles or stout bamboo canes inserted into the soil so that they form an inverted 'V' shape. Alternatively, use netting held by strong posts.

Dwarf beans may need support from short twigs. Tie the plants loosely at first to their supports. Once they start to grow, they will climb by themselves. Hoe the soil regularly and keep the plants clear of weeds. Copious watering is required in dry spells, and the flowers, when they appear, should be sprayed gently with water in the evenings to encourage pods to form. A thick moisture-retaining and weed-suppressing layer of damp peat can be put down around the plants in July. In late July and again in August feed the plants with liquid fertilizer. Once the plants have reached the tops of their supports remove their growing points to encourage the pods.

Above: The runner bean is a reliable and easy to grow vegetable, popular for its scarlet or white flowers.
Below: Garden peas are popular as a vegetable throughout the summer, and they will also freeze well.

Pests and diseases

Seeds may be eaten by slugs and millepedes. Mature plants may be attacked by aphids and capsids and botrytis (in wet summers).

Harvesting

Pick the pods when they are young and tender and do not wait until they are long and 'stringy' with the seeds bulging in the pods. By picking regularly, you should be able to harvest fresh for more than six weeks. Store the surplus crop by freezing or by salting.

Garden peas, petits pois and sugar peas (mangetout)

Planting to harvest time: 32 weeks for autumn sowings; 14 to 16 weeks for spring sowings.
Yields: 2kg to 4½kg (4lb to 10lb) to a 3m (10ft) row, depending on the variety.
Soil: Well-drained and rich in organic matter.

Ordinary garden peas come in two distinct types. There are round varieties which are very hardy and the quickest of all peas to mature. Then there are the wrinkle-seeded peas which are sweeter and heavier cropping. The French varieties of wrinkle-seeded pea are known as petit pois. Finally there are the sugar pea varieties which are eaten pods and all, or, as they are called in France, mangetout.

Sowing and planting

The soil should be enriched with compost and limed if necessary as peas prefer an alkaline soil. About a week before sowing give the soil a dressing of 56g/m² (2oz to the sq yd) of fertilizer and rake the soil back and forth to make it fine and crumbly. For peas in May and June, you should sow a round variety in either October or November and cover with cloches. For peas in June and July, you should sow a round or an early variety of wrinkle-seeded pea in March or April. For peas in August, sow a maincrop wrinkled variety in April or May. This is also the time to sow French petit pois and sugar peas. For peas in September, sow a wrinkled variety in June or July.

The technique of sowing peas is the same for all varieties. Make a drill 15cm (6in) wide and 5cm (2in) deep. The seeds are then placed by hand in three staggered rows in the drill so that each seed is approximately 7.5cm (3in) apart from its neighbours. Subsequent drills of peas should be a distance apart equal to the eventual height of the crop. So if you were growing a variety which is 75cm (30in) tall, your second drill would be 75cm (30in) away from the first.

Newly-sown seeds, unless covered with cloches, should be protected with plastic netting or wire netting guards. Hoe the soil regularly to keep it open and crumbly and to keep weeds under control. When the pea plants are 15cm (6in) high, insert twiggy branches along the outer sides of the drills to provide support. Dwarf varieties will not require any further assistance, but medium and tall varieties, especially those

of the sugar peas, will require plastic netting erected close to the drill for support. In June put down a 5cm (2in) moisture-retaining and weed-suppressing mulch of peat around the drills of peas. Water well during dry spells to swell the pods.

Pests and diseases
Aphids, birds and pea moth.

Harvesting
Pick the pods from the bottom of the plants when they appear well filled. The mangetout or sugar peas should be picked when the pods are fleshy, but before the shape of the peas can be seen in the pods. Store by freezing.

Sweetcorn

Sowing to harvest time: 12 to 16 weeks.
Yield: At least two cobs per plant.
Soil type: Any, provided it is enriched with compost.

If you have never tasted sweetcorn fresh from the garden, then you are in for a real treat when you harvest those first cobs.

Sowing and planting

The soil should be enriched with compost in winter. Then just before planting 112g/m² (4oz to the sq yd) of vegetable fertilizer should be lightly forked or raked in. The sweetcorn plants can be raised by sowing the seeds individually, 2.5cm (1in) deep in 7.5cm (3in) wide peat pots containing peat-based compost, between mid April and early May. The pots must be kept in either a greenhouse or indoors on a kitchen window sill until the risk of frost has passed in late May or early June. Alternatively, you can sow the seeds direct outdoors in mid May or early June. Two seeds should be sown together 2.5cm (1in) deep every 45cm (18in) along rows spaced 45cm (18in) apart. Since sweetcorn is pollinated by the wind, it is essential that you have at least four rows, no matter how short, so that you have a block of plants, providing the maximum amount of pollen. Once the outdoor seedlings are large enough to handle, thin to leave the strongest plant 45cm (18in) apart. The plants in peat pots should be set out 45cm (18in) apart each way in holes which have previously been filled with water, if the soil is not already moist. Since the roots of sweetcorn are very close to the surface, a moisture-retaining and weed-suppressing layer of peat is beneficial. In any case, do not hoe between the plants; far better to let the weeds grow than to destroy the roots of the sweetcorn.

Water copiously in dry spells.

Pests and diseases
None of any consequence.

Harvesting
The first sign that the cobs are ripening is when the silks at the tops of the green-sheathed cobs turn down. The next step is to make the thumb nail test. Pull back part of the sheath and squeeze a couple of corn grains between finger and thumbnail. If the liquid exuded is watery, the cob is not yet ripe. If the liquid is creamy, then you have cobs perfect for picking. If the liquid is doughy, then you are too late and the cobs are not fit for eating. The ripe cobs should be twisted free. Store by freezing.

Below top: Sweetcorn can be grown with success in a sunny position. Below bottom: The cobs of sweetcorn must be inspected for firmness and ripeness before picking.

Roots

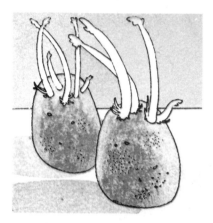

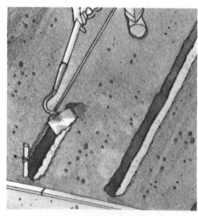

Above: Sowing and planting potatoes; top: put the tubers in egg boxes, tops upwards to encourage sprouting; centre: too much warmth or darkness causes shoots unfit for planting; bottom: dig V-shaped drills for planting sets. Above, right: Lifting a good crop of potatoes in summer.

Potato

Planting to harvest time: Early varieties, 14 weeks; maincrop varieties 20 to 22 weeks.

Yield: 6kg to 10kg (13lb to 22lb) to a 3m (10ft) row.

Soil: Most soils are suitable.

There are numerous varieties of potato. Some are white and floury and ideal for mashing or baking. Others are waxy and ideal for salads.

Sowing and planting

If possible, choose a sunny spot for potato growing and dig the soil in the autumn, incorporating compost if the soil is poor. You should obtain your seed potatoes in February and place them rose end (that is the bit with most of the shoots or 'eyes') uppermost in seed trays, or empty egg cartons, which should be placed in a cool, airy, light, but not sunny, spot such as a shed or garage so that the potatoes can start to sprout. A 9m (30ft) row or three 3m (10ft) rows will require 4kg (5lb) of seed potatoes.

Early varieties are planted between mid March and mid April, depending on the situation. Maincrop varieties are planted from mid April to mid May. When sow-ing, make V-shaped drills about 12.5cm (5in) deep and 60cm (24in) apart for early varieties, 45cm (30in) apart for maincrop varieties. The early varieties need be no more than 30cm (12in) apart in the drills; maincrop varieties should be 38cm (15in) apart. The seed potatoes should be set in the drills, rose end uppermost, and first covered with a little peat, compost or fine soil to prevent damage to the new shoots. The drills should then be filled in so that a slight ridge is left along the drills.

After planting, scatter vegetable fertilizer over the drills at the rate of 112g/m² (4oz to a sq yd). If there is still a risk of frost when the first shoots appear from the soil, draw a little earth over them for protection. When the shoots reach 22cm (9in) high, the process called earthing-up begins. Fork the soil lightly between the rows, and using your spade, pile the loose soil against the stems to produce a ridge 15cm (6in) high. Keep the weeds down between the rows with your hoe and flood with water whenever the weather is dry.

Pests and diseases

Aphids, scab, (grow resistant varieties) wart disease (grow resistant varieties), wireworm and blight. The last named is a disease peculiar to potatoes. The disease can be distinguished by brown markings on the leaves and by the fact that the haulm also collapses. The tubers develop sunken areas which are reddish brown beneath the surface. The preventative treatment for affected areas (as not all districts suffer from blight) is to spray with Bordeaux powder from early July at least three times at two-week intervals. As blight mainly affects maincrop potatoes, the solution in areas susceptible to the disease is to grow only early varieties which can be lifted before the July danger period.

Harvesting
Early varieties can be lifted when the flowers wither. Insert your fork into the soil well away from the haulm and then lift the haulm and its roots away from the row. Give the haulm a shake and most of the potatoes will fall away cleanly. When the haulms of maincrop varieties have withered in September or October, cut off the stems and remove them. Then wait for 10 days and lift the entire crop. The potatoes should be allowed to dry before storing them in hessian sacks, or in slatted wooden boxes in a dark, frost-free place.

Carrot
Sowing to harvest time: 15 weeks early varieties; 18 weeks maincrop.

Yield: Early varieties, 2kg (4½lb) to a 3m (10ft) row; maincrop, 4kg (9lb) to a 3m (10ft) row.

Soil: Deep and light, but any soil can be made suitable.

Forget what you may have heard about carrots requiring sandy soil. There are carrots to suit all soils. Round and short-rooted kinds are the best choice for stony soil or clay. Stump-rooted varieties will suit the majority of soils and those long-rooted types are grown on sandy soils.

Sowing and planting
Carrots do best on soil which has been well-prepared for a previous crop. Otherwise the soil should be prepared by deep digging in autumn or winter and dressed with 112g/m² (4oz to a sq yd) of granular vegetable fertilizer two weeks before sowing. Early varieties can be sown initially in March under cloches and at fortnightly intervals to mid-April. Sowings of maincrop varieties can begin in mid-April and continue at intervals until mid-July. Before sowing, rake the soil carefully to make it fine and crumbly. The drills should be just 0.5cm (¼in) deep and dusted lightly with Gamma-BHC as a precaution against carrot fly before sowing.

The seed should be sown as thinly as possible to cut down on the need for thinning later. If you wish to avoid this chore, use pelleted seed and place the pellets at 2.5cm (1in) intervals. Cover the drills with sifted soil and firm the surface with the flat head of a rake. Subsequent drills of early varieties should be 20cm (8in) apart; maincrop should be 30cm (12in) apart. Thin out the seedlings as soon as they are large enough to handle to 5cm (2in) apart and later to 10cm (4in) apart. The second thinnings will provide some usable little carrots. Water in dry spells and use the hoe to keep down weeds.

Pests and diseases
Aphid (leaves turn red and plants are stunted) and carrot fly.

Harvesting
The crop can be lifted as required. Maincrop carrots can be lifted for storage in October. The roots should be dried and the soil gently rubbed off. The foliage should be cut off 1cm (about ½in) above the crowns and the carrots stored in layers in boxes with dry peat between the layers. The store must not be damp or soft rot will result.

Rich in vitamin A carrots are especially good for children.

Right: The swede is a good winter root vegetable which stores well.

Below: Salsify is often called the vegetable oyster owing to its delicate flavour.

Swede

Sowing to harvest time: 20 to 24 weeks.
Yield: 5kg (11lb) to a 3m (10ft) row.
Soil: Any

In the North of England and Scotland, mashed swedes are considered almost a delicacy. They are also called in those areas 'turnips'. The beauty of swedes is that they can be harvested in October or later and so provide a source of vegetables all winter.

Sowing and planting
Rake over the soil occupied by a previous crop and work in a dressing of 56g to 84g/m² (2oz to 3oz to a sq yd) of vegetable fertilizer. In cold districts, the seed can be sown in May. However, in warmer areas it is better to wait until June or the beginning of July. Sow the seed thinly in drills 1.3cm (½in) apart and thin as soon as the seedlings are large enough to handle. If you want 'spring greens', leave part of a row unthinned. Keep watered and free from weeds.

Pests and diseases
Flea beetles, root fly, and club root.

Harvesting
Swedes can be lifted from October onwards for use when required. In mild areas the crop can be left in the ground over winter. Elsewhere the roots can be dug up, dried, the tops twisted off and stored in boxes of dried peat.

Turnips

Sowing to harvest time: 7 to 14 weeks.
Yield: 4kg (9lb) to a 3m (10ft) row.
Soil: Any.

Turnips come in all shapes and sizes and in various colours from pure white to yellow; there are turnips with purple skins and others with skins of greenish gold.

Sowing and planting
The soil for turnips should be dug over in winter and limed if necessary. Alternatively, you can sow on the land occupied by a previous crop. Before sowing the soil should be dressed with 56g to 84g/m² (2 to 3oz to a sq yd) of vegetable fertilizer and raked level. The aim should be to produce a seed bed which is firm and yet has a fine crumbly appearance.

Early turnips can be sown in succession from mid-April onwards in drills 1.3cm (½in) deep with 38cm (15in) between the drills. Maincrop turnips can be sown in late July to mid-August for harvesting in October for storage over the winter. For 'turnip tops' sow thinly in late August and do not thin out.

Early and maincrop seedlings should be thinned initially to 7.5cm (3in) apart when they have developed their first rough turnip leaves. A couple of weeks later, thin again to leave the turnips 15cm (6in) apart.

These thinnings can be eaten. Hoe frequently to keep the soil open and free from weeds. Water copiously if the weather is dry.

Pests and diseases

Flea beetles, root fly and club root.

Harvesting

Early varieties should be lifted as required. They are at their best when about the size of a tennis ball. In October the maincrop can be lifted with a fork, dried, the tops twisted off and the roots stored in boxes of dried peat.

Salsify/scorzonera

Sowing to harvest time: 26 to 30 weeks.
Yield: 3kg (6½lb) to a 3m (10ft) row.
Soil: Any.

Salsify, which is white-skinned, has a distinctive, somewhat fishy taste. Hence its other name; the vegetable oyster. Scorzonera, which has black skin, has a similar flavour and both vegetables make delicious additions to winter meals.

Sowing and planting

The soil for both salsify and scorzonera should be prepared by deep digging. If possible, remove any large stones which could cause the roots to fork. Two weeks before sowing (early April for salsify, late April for scorzonera) give the soil a 112g/m² (4oz to a sq yd) dressing of general fertilizer and rake the soil to make it fine and crumbly. Sow the seeds thinly in 1.3cm (½in) deep drills 30cm (12in) apart. Later thin the seedlings to 23cm (9in) apart in the rows. The plants should be kept well watered and free from weeds. It is a good idea to put down a moisture-retaining and weed-suppressing layer of peat to cut out the need to hoe near the roots which bleed easily if damaged.

Pests and diseases

None of any consequence.

Harvesting

In mild areas both salsify and scorzonera can be harvested throughout the winter as required. Otherwise the crop can be lifted in the autumn, the top growth twisted off and the roots stored in boxes of dry peat in a cool, frost-free shed or garage.

Parsnip

Sowing to harvest time: 30 to 34 weeks.
Yield: 4kg (9lb) to a 3m (10ft) row.
Soil: Deep rich, fairly light soil, but most soils with correct varieties are suitable.

There are three distinct varieties of parsnips. The short-rooted kinds are the best choice for stony soils or where the parsnip disease, canker, is troublesome. The intermediate varieties are a good choice for general cultivation as they offer top yields combined with first-class flavour. The long-rooted types are only for gardens with ideal soil conditions.

Sowing and planting

The soil should be dug deeply in winter. Then before sowing break down the soil thoroughly with a fork, give the plot a dressing of 112g/m² (4oz to a sq yd) of vegetable fertilizer and rake it level. The seed should be sown in March or April, depending on the weather and where you live, in drills of 1.3cm (1½in) deep with 30cm (12in) between them. Place the seeds three to a cluster at 20cm (8in) intervals along the drills and later thin out to leave just one plant at each position. Hoe to keep the soil free from weeds and water when necessary.

Pests and diseases

Aphids, carrot fly, leaf miner and canker. (Canker is root rot, grow resistant varieties).

Harvesting

The roots are ready for lifting when the foliage dies down in the autumn. Lift as required. The roots can remain in the soil over the winter as frost improves the flavour. Alternatively lift some roots and store in boxes of dry peat for use during unfavourable lifting weather.

Above: The turnip is delicious if lifted when young and tender, and will also store well for the winter months.

Below: Parsnips have a delicious, individual taste. They are at their best served with butter.

Onion family

Above: The leek is a hardy vegetable. It thrives in ordinary soil and can be left in the ground over winter.

Opposite page, above: Onions can be plaited together with raffia and stored hanging up in a garage or out-house where dry air can circulate around them.

such as early peas or potatoes. If not, work in some well-rotted compost or peat and give the soil a dressing of vegetable fertilizer at the rate of 112g/m² (4oz to a sq yd) two weeks before planting. The seed should be sown outdoors in a nursery bed in a drill 1.3cm (½in) deep between early March and mid-April. The seedlings are ready for transplanting in June or July when they are 20cm (8in) high. They should be set out in rows 30cm (12in) apart with 15cm (6in) between the plants.

Transplanting calls for a special procedure; 15cm (6in) deep holes are made for the leeks with a dibber or stick; the plants are dropped in the holes; the holes are then filled with water which settles the soil around the roots. There is no need to fill the holes with soil. The plants should be kept weed free and water should be given whenever the weather is dry. Soil can be drawn up against the stems of the plants as they develop if you wish your leeks well blanched.

Pests and diseases
Virtually none.

Harvesting
Lift the leeks out of the soil with a fork when they are the thickness of a finger. Since leeks can remain in the soil throughout the winter months, harvest as required.

Onion: bulb varieties, spring and pickling
Planting/sowing to harvest time: Onions raised from seed take 44 weeks if August sown, 22 weeks if spring sown. Onions raised from sets take 18 weeks. Spring onions take 10 to 12 weeks. Pickling onions take 22 weeks.
Yield: 3½kg (8lb) of bulbs from seed or sets to a 3m (10ft) row and 1kg (2lb) spring onions to a 3m (10ft) row.
Soil: Well drained, light and rich in organic matter.

Onions are a most useful crop as they store so easily. The bulbs also have possibly more culinary uses than any other vegetable.

Sowing and planting
The soil should be prepared by digging in plenty of compost and dressing with

Leek
Sowing to harvest time: 35 weeks, early varieties; 45 weeks, late varieties.
Yield: 5kg (1lb) to a 3m (1ft) row.
Soil: Any.

The leek thrives even in districts where the growing conditions are poor. So little can go wrong that even someone new to gardening can hardly fail to achieve success.

Sowing and planting
Ideally the soil for leeks should have been enriched with compost for a previous crop

vegetable fertilizer at the rate of 112g/m² (4oz to a sq yd). When the soil is dry, tread it firm and then rake it carefully to produce a fine crumbly appearance. In mild districts the seed can be sown in August to produce tiny bulbs for transplanting in March and a crop in July. Elsewhere the seed can be sown in March or April to produce a late August or September crop.

The seed should be sown very thinly 1.3cm ($\frac{1}{2}$in) deep in rows 30cm (12in) apart. Seedlings from an August sowing should be transplanted to 15cm (6in) apart with 30cm (12in) between the rows. Spring sown onions should be thinned first to 5cm (2in) and later to 15cm (6in) apart, retaining 30cm (12in) between the rows. The thinnings can be used as 'spring onions' for salads. However, it is better to use a special variety for this purpose. The seeds should be sown as for ordinary onions, except that the rows need be just 15cm (6in) apart and the seedlings are not thinned. With 'spring onions', successional sowings at approximately fortnightly intervals are essential to produce plenty of delicately flavoured young plants. Pickling onions are sown in the same way in rows 25cm (10in) apart and like 'spring onions' are not thinned.

To produce a crop of onions from the little bulbs called 'sets', the soil should be

prepared carefully as for seed sowing. Each bulb should be pushed into the soil so that its neck is barely visible. The bulbs should be 15cm (6in) apart with 30cm (12in)

Below: Bending over the tops of the onions hastens ripening; the onions are left out until they are firm and fully ripe.

between the rows. All onions should be kept free from weeds and watered regularly. An additional feed of 56g/m² (2oz to the sq yd) of vegetable fertilizer can be given in May and hoed in lightly to increase the size of the bulbs. Snap off any flower heads which may appear. Stop watering as the bulbs begin to ripen and draw the soil away from the bulbs to enable the sun to get at them.

Pests and diseases
Onion fly (but sets are generally free from attack). Birds may pull sets from the ground (the remedy is to snip off loose skin from the neck of the bulbs before planting).

Harvesting
When the leaves have toppled over and started to yellow, the crop can be lifted and allowed to dry on a wire netting cradle a few inches from the ground. Store by plaiting with raffia or by hanging in plastic netting in shed or garage.

Shallot
Planting to harvest time: 18 to 25 weeks.
Yield: $4\frac{1}{2}$kg (10lb) to a 3m (10ft) row.
Soil: Well-drained and rich in organic matter.

Shallots are very easy to grow and some people find that they make a mild alternative to onions. They are also good for pickling. Unlike onions which produce a single bulb, shallots grow into clumps of little bulbs around the original 'set'.

Planting
In late autumn or early winter dig over the soil and fork in compost. Early in February give the soil a dressing of 56g/m² (2oz to the sq yd) of vegetable fertilizer and hoe this in – at the same time attempting to get the soil fine and crumbly. In mid-February or before mid-March, push the bulbs into the soil so that their necks are barely visible. The bulbs should be 15cm to 20cm (6in to 8in) apart in rows 30cm (12in) apart. Hoe carefully to avoid damage to the bulbs and water only when absolutely necessary. In June scrape some soil away from the bulb clusters to expose them to the sun and so assist ripening.

Pests and disease
Shallots suffer from the same problems as onions.

Harvesting
As soon as the foliage has yellowed in June or July, dig up the shallots and dry them on a wire netting cradle a few inches from the ground. When dried, rub off any dead foliage and loose skin. The tiniest bulbs can be put aside for next year's crop. The others can be stored in plastic netting in shed or garage.

Propagation
The tiny bulbs too small for cooking can be used to provide the following year's supply of shallots.

Below right: Shallots are mild members of the onion family and popular for pickling.

Salad vegetables

Lettuce
Sowing to harvest time: 10 to 14 weeks.
Yield: 10 to 30 heads, depending on the variety, to a 3m (10ft) row.
Soil: Well-drained and rich in humus.

There are two types of lettuce: cabbage lettuce and cos lettuce. The cabbage types in turn can be sub-divided into 'butter-heads' with soft, floppy leaves, and 'crisp hearts' which have crisper leaves than the butterheads and are more resistant to heat and less liable to run to seed. Cos lettuces are upright and have crisp self-folding leaves. They do not run readily to seed and their leaves remain much cleaner during sudden summer downpours.

Sowing and planting
The soil for lettuces must contain plenty of matter if solid-hearted plants are to be produced. Two weeks before sowing or planting out the soil should be dressed with 56g/m² (2oz to a sq yd) of granular vegetable fertilizer.

For a summer crop sow outdoors in succession from late March to late July to produce lettuces from June to October. For an early winter crop sow a forcing variety in August and cover with cloches from September to provide lettuces in November and December. Forcing varieties can also be sown in the greenhouse from August to October to provide lettuces from November to April.

For a spring crop outdoors, sow a hardy winter variety at the end of August or in September and harvest in May. For lettuces outdoors in April, sow a forcing variety at the beginning of October and cover with cloches. The seed can be sown thinly in short drills, 1.3cm ($\frac{1}{2}$in) deep and transplanted later to 10cm to 30cm (4in to 12in) apart, depending on the variety. Alternatively, you can use pelleted seed and place the individual seeds in the drills 5cm (2in) apart with 10cm to 30cm (4in to 12in) between the rows, and later thin out to the required spacing. This method gives faster results as lettuces are not over keen on being moved. Another possibility is to raise the plants indoors and to transplant outdoors when they can be handled easily.

Pests and diseases
Aphids, birds, millipedes, root aphids, slugs and botrytis (grey mould).

Harvesting
Lift from the garden as required.

Below left: Lettuces can be covered with cloches to provide lettuce late in the year.
Below right: The crisp heart lettuce is more resistant to heat and less liable to run to seed.

Right: Blanching endive under flower-pots.
Below right: Blanched chicons are generally used in salads, but are also delicious braised or made into soup.

Endive

Sowing to harvest time: 14 to 20 weeks.
Yield: 12 heads to a 3m (10ft) row.
Soil: Well-drained and rich in humus.

Endive looks just like a curly headed lettuce but tastes less bland. Since it is generally in season from late August until early winter, its main advantage is that, being hardier than most lettuces, it provides a very useful contribution to autumn salads.

Sowing and planting

The soil should be prepared by digging in plenty of compost and dressing with 56g/m² (2oz to a sq yd) of granular vegetable fertilizer about two weeks before sowing. The seeds can be sown thinly at intervals from June to August in drills 1.3cm (½in) deep and 30cm (12in) apart. As soon as the seedlings can be handled easily, they should be thinned to 23cm (9in) apart. As endive seedlings do not transplant readily, the thinnings should be discarded. The crop benefits from two additional feeds at intervals during its growing period of 28g (1oz) of nitrate of soda, sulphate of amonia or nitro chalk to each 3m (10ft) row. Some people prefer blanched endive to reduce the plant's bitterness. This can be achieved by covering the heads for 14 days with large flower pots to exclude the light. Alternatively, the leaves can be tied up together using raffia.

Pests and diseases

Virtually trouble free.

Harvesting

Lift as required.

Chicory

Sowing to harvest time: 16 to 18 weeks.
Yield: 12 chicon-producing roots to a 3m (10ft) row.
Soil: Well-drained and rich in organic matter.

Chicory is grown for neither its leaves nor roots, but the blanched chicons which are produced by forcing the roots in warmth and darkness.

Sowing and planting

Chicory can be sown on soil which was well fed for a previous crop, or you can dig the plot deeply in spring and enrich it with plenty of garden compost. Dress the area with 168g/m² (6oz to a sq yd) with carbonate of lime, unless the soil is already chalky or limy. Sow the seeds in late April or early May on a prepared seed bed, 1.3cm (½in) deep in drills 38cm (15in) apart. When the seedlings have three leaves, thin to 23cm (9in) apart. Keep the plants weed-free and well watered.

Forcing and harvesting

In late October or November when the leaves are dying back, lift the roots carefully. They should be 5cm to 7.5cm (2in to 3in) thick at the top and around 25cm (10in) long. Trim them to 20cm (8in) and cut away all the leaves above the crown. Store the roots in a cool, frost-free place.

Only a few roots should be forced at a time to produce chicons. Pack five roots in a 23cm (9in) diameter plastic flower pot containing sand or fairly moist seed compost. Cover with another 23cm (9in) pot and place in a dark spot where the temperature is 10° to 13°C (50° to 55°F). Cut the chicons about an hour before they are required and when they are 12.5cm to 15cm (5in to 6in) long.

Pests and diseases

Slugs.

Mustard and Cress

Sowing to harvest time: 15 days for mustard. 18 days for cress.
Yield: 225g (8oz) from an area 25cm by 25cm (10in by 10in).
Soil type: Fine and moisture-retentive.

Mustard and cress are usually grown together and used in their seedling stage for salads and sandwiches.

Sowing

Although mustard and cress can be grown outdoors, it is far better to sow the seeds indoors in succession to provide usable quantities of the vegetables as required. Fill small plastic seed trays or flower pots with moist seed compost and scatter the seeds over the top. Cover the containers with newspaper until the seeds germinate. Then place the containers on a sunny window ledge. Keep well watered. The vegetables can be provided all year round in this way by indoor sowings. Outdoors the sowings should be made on fine soil in the same way from April to September.

Pests and diseases
Virtually trouble free.

Harvesting
Cut the seedlings with scissors when they are about 5cm (2in) high.

Beetroot

Sowing to harvest time: 12 to 18 weeks.
Yield: 3kg (6½lb) to a 3m (10ft) row, early varieties; 4kg (9lb) to a 3m (10ft) row, maincrop.
Soil: Fertile and light.

Beetroot is a welcome addition to any salad. As well as the normal dark red beets, there are golden beets and white beets, which are equally delicious.

Sowing and planting
The soil should be dug over in winter, and about two weeks before sowing dressed with vegetable fertilizer at the rate of 112g/m^2 (4oz to a sq yd). Sow the seeds very thinly 2.5cm (1in) deep in rows 30cm (12in) apart. Successional sowings can be made from April to June for a steady supply. The maincrop for winter storage should be sown in early June. As soon as the seedlings can be handled easily, thin out to 5cm (2in) apart. Later thin to 10cm (4in) apart and use the thinnings for salads. Hoe regularly to keep down weeds and water when necessary to prevent the roots from splitting. The maincrop is best surrounded by a layer of moist peat in summer.

Pests and diseases
Leaf miners.

Harvesting
Lift small beetroots as required. The maincrop should be lifted in early October and the roots dried and any loose soil rubbed off. Twist off the foliage and store the roots in boxes of dried peat. The store should be a frost-free shed or garage.

*Above: Mustard and cress are a bright addition to sandwiches and often a tasteful finishing touch for a dish being brought to the table.
Below: Beetroot is a sweet salad vegetable with a high food value.*

Above: Radishes are easy and quick to grow giving a high yield with minimum effort.
Right: Celery, long thought to be a difficult vegetable to grow because of the trenching and blanching involved, is in fact not difficult or time-consuming. Self-blanching varieties have made growing celery much simpler.

Radish

Sowing to harvest time: 4 to 6 weeks; summer varieties; 10 to 12 weeks, winter varieties.

Yield: 2kg ($4\frac{1}{2}$lb) to a 3m (10ft) row, summer varieties; $4\frac{1}{2}$kg (10lb) to a 3m (10ft) row, winter varieties.

Soil: Well-drained and rich in humus.

Sowing and planting

Unless the soil has been fed for a previous crop, dress with vegetable fertilizer at the rate of 56g/m² (2oz to a sq yd). Summer varieties should be sown in succession from March to early June in drills 1.3m ($\frac{1}{2}$in) deep and 15cm (6in) apart. Sow the seed sparingly to cut out the need for thinning. If overcrowding does take place, thin the seedlings to 2.5cm to 5cm (1in to 2in) apart. Winter varieties should be sown from late July to mid-August in drills 23cm (9in) apart and later thinned to 15cm (6in) apart. Water thoroughly in dry spells as fast-growing radishes never recover from drought.

Pests and diseases

Flea beetles and root fly.

Harvesting

Lift summer varieties while they are still young and tender. Winter varieties can be left in the soil and lifted during the winter as required, but it is better to lift them in late October; remove the loose soil, twist off the top growth and store the roots in boxes of dry peat. The store should be a frost-free area such as a toolshed, workshop or garage.

Celery

Planting to harvest time: 28 to 34 weeks.

Yield: 6.5kg (14lb) to a 3m (10ft) row.

Soil: Well-drained, but moisture-retentive.

Crisp celery stalks are useful for salads from late summer to spring. They are also splendid as a vegetable in soups and stews.

Sowing and planting

There are two types of celery: trench varieties, which provide stems from autumn to spring, and the self-blanching varieties which are ready from late summer and which are milder in flavour. These latter varieties have made celery growing much simpler. The plot for self-blanching varieties should be dug over in April, adding as much compost as possible. Trench varieties require a special trench which is also prepared in April, by digging out the soil 30cm (12in) deep and 38cm (15in) wide for a single row of plants, and 45cm (18in) wide for a double row. The trench should then have liberal quantities

of compost forked into the soil in the bottom. Soil taken from the trench should be returned so that the level is raised to 15cm (6in) from the top of the trench. The remaining soil should be used to make mounds 7.5m (3in) high on either side of the trench.

In April, sow the seeds in compost indoors and prick off when 1.3cm (½in) high into boxes of potting compost. Keep the plants growing steadily and transplant outdoors in June or July. With the self-blanching varieties, plant in a square on level ground 23cm (9in) apart each way. With the trench varieties, space the plants 25cm (10in) in a single row down the middle of the 38cm (15in) wide trench; if planting a double row in a 45cm (18in) wide trench, space them 30cm (12in) apart with 25cm (10in) between the rows. Do not stagger the rows, as setting the plants in pairs makes them easier to earth up later.

After you have finished planting, flood the trench with water. Two or three times in July and August give the plants a feed with vegetable fertilizer at the rate of 56g/m² (2oz to a sq yd). When the trench varieties are 25cm (10in) high, blanching can begin. Remove any side shoots, wrap the stems in newspaper collars, tie loosely and pile the soil in the mounds at the sides of the trench against the collars. In late September complete earthing up so that only the foliage of the plants is showing.

Pests and diseases

Celery fly (grubs cause brown blisters – spray with malathion or trichlorphon), aphids, leaf miners, slugs and leaf spot (brown rusty spots on leaves and stems – spray with Bordeaux powder every two to three weeks).

Harvesting

Lift the self-blanching varieties as you need them. The trench varieties are ready about nine weeks from the start of earthing up. Remove plants from the end of the row as required, taking care to avoid disturbing neighbouring plants.

If trench varieties are grown, this facilitates blanching, and as the plants grow they are earthed up until only the foliage is showing.

vegetable fruits

Above: Given suitable conditions tomatoes will give an abundant crop. Below: Home-grown greenhouse cucumber: here the shoots have been tied up and the male flowers removed.

Tomato

Sowing to harvest time: 18 weeks, greenhouse varieties; 20 weeks, outdoor varieties.

Yield: 4kg to 5kg (9lb to 11lb) per plant indoors; 2kg (4½lb) per plant outdoors.

Soil: Compost gives best results indoors; outdoors, plants need rich, moisture-retentive soil, or you can use compost in pots or plastic growing bags.

Tomatoes are fairly easy to grow, provided that you choose the most suitable varieties for the conditions. Outdoors, bush varieties give the best results in cold districts. They also have the added advantage that they can be covered with cloches to speed the ripening of the fruit.

Sowing and planting

If a heated greenhouse is available (minimum night temperature, 10 °C or 50°F) seed can be sown in December to raise plants for setting out in March. However if the greenhouse is unheated, the seed should not be sown until mid-March to produce plants for setting out in late April or early May for a July crop.

The seed to produce plants for outdoor growing should be sown in late March or early April. At the appropriate time, raise the seeds by sowing two seeds 1.3cm (½in) deep in peat-based compost in 7.5cm (3in) wide peat pots. Once the seedlings have their true tomato leaves remove the weaker seedlings from each pot. As a temperature of around 17°C (55°F) is required for successful germination in a week to 12 days, the ideal spot initially for the peat pots is a warm cupboard indoors.

When the time comes to put the plants in the greenhouse, plant peat pots and all in compost-filled growing bags or in 23cm (9in) wide ring pots filled with potting compost and standing on a 15cm (6in) thick aggregate base. It is not a good idea to grow tomatoes in the greenhouse soil as this leads to disease. Tie the main stem loosely to a bamboo cane or wind it loosely up a firmly supported vertical string. Side shoots should be removed when they are 2.5cm (1in) long. Water frequently and start to feed once a week with tomato fertilizer once the first truss of fruit has set.

For tomatoes outdoors the soil should be well prepared by digging in plenty of compost and dressing with 112g/m² (4oz to a sq yd) of vegetable fertilizer. Otherwise use compost filled growing bags or 23cm (9in) plastic pots. Set the plants outdoors in June when they are 15cm (5in) tall, with 45cm (18in) between the plants and 60cm (2ft) between subsequent rows. Standard varieties will require the support of 1.50cm (5ft) canes; bush varieties need no support.

Watering, feeding and the removal of sideshoots should be carried out as with greenhouse tomatoes, except in the case of bush tomatoes where the removal of sideshoots is unnecessary. With the standard varieties, the tops of the plants should be removed after the fourth truss to encourage all of the crop to ripen.

Pests and diseases

Aphids, white fly (spray underside of leaves with malathion and repeat at seven day intervals), blight (leaves and fruit turn brown – spray with Bordeaux powder from early July), and damping off (seedlings).

Harvesting

Gather the fruit when it is well-coloured. Greenhouse tomatoes can be left on the plants until the first frosts. Outdoor fruit is best picked by late September and the remaining green fruit allowed to ripen on a window sill. Freeze the surplus crop.

Cucumber: indoor and outdoor or 'frame' and 'ridge.'

Sowing to harvest time: 10 to 12 weeks indoors; 12 to 14 weeks outdoors.
Yield: 25 fruits per plant.
Soil: Well-drained and rich in organic matter outdoors; compost in pots or growing bags indoors.

Sowing and planting

Varieties for heated greenhouses (minimum temperature 18°C – 65°F) can be sown in February. All female varieties require a minimum night temperature of 21°C (70°F) and are beyond the scope – and pocket – of many amateurs. For unheated greenhouses, frames and outdoors, sow in April, two seeds 1.3cm ($\frac{1}{2}$in) deep in 7.5cm (3in) wide peat pots containing peat-based compost. If the pots are stood in a hot, dark cupboard, germination will take place in 4 to 9 days. Once the plants have developed their first true cucumber leaves, thin out to leave one plant in each pot.

In mid May the plants for the greenhouse can be set in growing bags, or 23cm (9in) wide plastic pots containing peat-based potting compost, and trained up a vertical wire or cane. The top should be removed when the plant reaches the desired height. Train the side shoots along wires attached horizontally to the greenhouse glazing bars. The tip of each side shoot should be removed at a point two leaves beyond a female flower. With greenhouse cucumber varieties all male flowers should be removed as fertilized fruit is bitter. Female flowers can be distinguished by the miniature cucumber behind their petals. Keep the soil nicely moist, but not soaking, and feed every two weeks with a liquid general fertilizer after the first fruits swell.

Outdoor cucumbers can be grown in compost-filled growing bags or in soil specially prepared for them. Take out holes for the plants 30cm wide and 30cm deep (12in by 12in) with 60cm (2ft) between the holes. Then fill the holes with a mixture of well-rotted compost and soil. Top dress the bed with vegetable fertilizer at the rate of 112g/m2 (4oz to a sq yd). A second row of compost-filled holes should be 90cm (3ft) apart from the first. Such planting holes can be covered in cold districts with frames or cloches.

The plants should have their growing points removed when they have seven leaves. Side shoots will then develop and these should be pinched out at four leaves. Once fruit has formed, the fruiting laterals should have their tops removed at a point two leaves beyond the tiny cucumber. Keep the soil moist at all times, but water around the plants not over them as this helps to prevent stems and fruit rotting. Feed fortnightly with liquid general fertilizer once the first fruits have formed and support ripening fruits on pieces of tile or board to keep them clean and free from the attention of slugs. Do not remove male flowers as outdoor cucumbers require to be fertilized to produce fruit.

Pests and diseases

Capsids (tattered holes in leaves – spray with derris), red spider (leaves marked with pale patches – spray with derris), slugs (protect plants at planting out time) and botrytis.

Marrow, courgette, pumpkin and squash

Sowing to harvest time: 10 to 14 weeks.
Yield: Varies enormously with type: but 6kg (13lb) courgettes to a 3m (10ft) row; marrows and squashes yield at least 2kg (4$\frac{1}{2}$lb) per plant and pumpkins 3 to 5 fruits per plant, weighing 9 to 14kg (20lb to 30lb) each.
Soil: Well-drained and very rich in organic matter.

Marrows come in bush types and trailing kinds, yielding fruit which can be sausage-shaped, oval or almost round, Courgettes are really varieties of marrows which produce small fruits over a long period. Squashes, or custard marrows, are an American vegetable, producing fruit which is roundish and varies from 7.5cm (3in) to 25cm (10in) in diameter. Finally there are the pumpkins and thick-skinned types called winter squashes which store well.

Sowing and planting

Individual compost-filled holes should be prepared for each plant. Dig out these holes 30cm (12in) wide and 30cm (12in) deep 60 cm (24in) apart for bush types and 1.20m (4ft) apart at least for trailing vegetables. Then fill the holes with a mixture of compost and soil and give the bed a dressing of vegetable fertilizer at the rate of 112g/m2 (4oz to a sq yd). When the risk of frost has passed, generally late May, sow three seeds 2.5cm deep on each compost filled hole. Put down slug pellets as a safety measure. As soon as the seedlings have two true rough leaves, thin out to leave just one plant at each position. The soil must be kept moist at all times. Water copiously around

Above top: The marrow has an attractive yellow flower seen here with the young fruit.
Above: Courgettes with regular cutting will produce small fruits over a long period of time.

65

Top: Red peppers are popular for adding colour to food.
Bottom: The fast-growing aubergine.

the plants but not over them. Bush types may need support with bamboo canes when they are 90cm (3ft) high. The tips of the main shoots of trailing types should be pinched off when they reach 90cm (3ft) long. Once the fruits start to swell, feed with a liquid general fertilizer every fortnight. Weeds are best prevented, rather than removed, by putting down a 2.5cm (1in) thick layer of moist peat. In cold districts plants can be covered with cloches and frames.

Pests and diseases
Capsids (tattered holes in leaves – spray with derris), red spider (leaves marked with pale patches – spray with derris), slugs and botrytis.

Harvesting
Cut courgettes when they are 10cm (4in) long for use as required; marrows are best when 25cm (10in) long. Constant cutting is essential to prolong fruiting. Marrows, pumpkins and squashes required for winter storage should be allowed to mature on the plants and cut just before the first frosts are expected. Store on slatted shelves or in plastic nets slung between beams in a cool frost-free shed or garage.

Aubergine (egg plant)
Sowing to harvest time: 22 to 26 weeks.
Yield: 4 fruits per plant.
Soil: John Innes No. 3 compost or peat-based compost in a growing bag. With the introduction of faster ripening varieties, even weekend gardeners can achieve remarkable success in growing aubergines.

Sowing and planting
Sow the seeds in February or March singly, 1.3cm ($\frac{1}{2}$in) deep, in 7.5cm (3in) wide peat pots, containing peat-based compost, and keep in a temperature indoors as close to 21°C (70°F) as possible. The plants should have their growing tips pinched out when they are 12.5cm to 15cm (5in to 6in) high to encourage the formation of two leading shoots. If the plants are becoming obviously too large for their pots, they can be planted, peat pots included, in 12.5cm (5in) diameter plastic pots containing peat-based compost. In mid May the plants can be set out, four to a growing bag, in the greenhouse. If you wish to have the plants outdoors, move them to 17.5cm (7in) wide pots containing John Innes No. 3 compost in early June and stand the pots in a sunny sheltered spot.

The plants will require stakes. Remove any side-shoots as they appear and feed with liquid general fertilizer every fortnight. The fruits vary in size and shape from roundish to sausage shaped and are usually a very deep purple. Allow only four fruits to develop on each plant. Regular spraying with water will encourage the fruits to set.

Pests and diseases
Generally trouble free.

Harvesting
Pick the aubergines from late July onwards while the bloom is still on their skins, and they are slightly soft. As the shine disappears, the fruit tends to become bitter. Store by freezing.

Capsicum, sweet pepper, red and green pepper
Sowing to harvest time: 20 to 26 weeks.
Yield: Depends on variety, but generally 0.68kg to 0.96kg (1$\frac{1}{2}$lb to 2lb) per plant.
Soil: John Innes No. 2 compost or peat-based compost in a growing bag. Capsicums, sweet peppers, green peppers and red peppers are all the same vegetable and come in all shapes and sizes.

Sowing and planting
Sow the seeds in March or April singly, 1.3cm ($\frac{1}{2}$in) deep, in 7.5cm (3in) wide peat pots, containing peat-based compost, and keep in a temperature indoors as close to 18°C (65°F) as possible. When the plants are 12.5cm to 15cm (5in to 6in) tall, pinch out their growing tips to encourage the formation of two leading shoots. If the plants become too large for their peat pots, they can be planted, peat pots included, in 12.5cm (5in) diameter plastic pots containing peat-based compost.

In mid-May the plants can be set out, four to a growing bag, in the greenhouse. If you wish to have the plants outdoors, move them to 17.5cm (7in) wide pots containing John Innes No. 2 compost in early June and stand the pots in a sunny sheltered spot.

The plants will require stakes. Spray the plants gently with water during the flowering period to encourage fruit to form. Give weak feeds of liquid general fertilizer at fortnightly intervals from the time the fruits first appear until they show colour.

Pests and diseases
Aphids, but generally trouble-free.

Harvesting
Start to pick the fruits when they are still green – unless you want some red peppers. Store the surplus crop by freezing.

Herbs

Even with a wide variety of vegetables there are still some vital ingredients missing – herbs. Here are six plants which take up little space and are so invaluable in the kitchen for flavouring food.

Chives
Hardy perennial
Spread: 20cm by 30cm (8in by 12in)
Position: Sun or slight shade.
Soil: Any, provided that it is well drained.
Sowing
Sow in March and April in rows 1cm ($\frac{1}{2}$in) deep. Thin seedlings to 15cm (6in) apart. Seed can also be sown indoors and one seedling placed in each 13cm (5in) pot.
Harvesting
Cut leaves close to the ground to encourage further growth. Remove flowers.
Storing
Leaves may be deep frozen.

Mint
Perennial
Spread: 30cm by 45cm (12in by 18in).
Position: Sun or partial shade.
Soil: Fertile and moist.
Planting
In spring or autumn plant pieces of root in 25cm or 30cm (10in or 12in) diameter clay pots containing good soil or John Innes No. 3 compost and sink the pots in the garden soil so that the rims are level with the soil surface.
Harvesting
Gather the leaves as required.
Storing
Freezing or drying.

Parsley
Biennial, but best treated as an annual.
Spread: 25cm by 25cm (10in by 10in)
Position: Sunny and sheltered.
Soil: Rich and moist.
Sowing: Sow in March and April for summer and autumn harvest; sow in July for winter and spring. Sow the seed very thinly in drills no more than 6mm ($\frac{1}{4}$in) deep. Germination takes three to six weeks. Thin the seedlings to 23cm (9in) apart. Seedlings can also be planted in 13cm (5in) diameter pots with suitable compost.
Harvesting
Cut as required.

Storing
Freezing or drying.

Rosemary
Hardy evergreen shrub
Spread: 60cm to 150cm by 60cm to 150cm (2ft to 5ft by 2ft to 5ft).
Position: Sunny and sheltered.
Soil: Light and well-drained.
Sowing and planting
Sow seeds in March outdoors 6mm ($\frac{1}{4}$in) deep. Thin as required and transplant to a final spacing of 60cm (24in) apart.
Harvesting
Cut sprigs as required.
Storing
Unnecessary as rosemary is evergreen.

Sage
Shrub with a useful life of three years.
Spread: 30cm to 60cm by 45cm (12in to 24in by 18in).
Position: Warm and sunny.
Soil: Any, provided that it is well drained.
Sowing and planting: Sow the seeds 6mm ($\frac{1}{4}$in) deep in a nursery bed in early summer, thin and move the plants to their final positions the following spring 60cm (24in) apart.
Harvesting
Gather leaves as required.
Storing
Leaves for drying should be picked in May.

Thyme
Shrub/herbaceous perennial, with a useful life of three years.
Spread: 23cm by 23cm (9in by 9in).
Position: Full sun.
Soil: Any, provided that it is well drained.
Planting
Nursery-grown stock should be set out 23cm (9in) apart in March or April. Alternatively, each plant can be accommodated in a 15cm (6in) diameter pot containing John Innes No. 3 compost.

After three years the plants can be lifted in spring and divided and small, healthy pieces replanted.
Harvesting
Pick the leaves as required.
Storing
Dry leaves picked before the flowers appear in June.

Herbs are satisfying to grow in the kitchen garden both for their pleasant smell while growing and the pleasure of using fresh herbs in cooking. Winter supplies can be assured by harvesting into bunches and hanging them to dry in a warm place.

THE FRUITS
OF SUCCESS

Growing fruit in your garden will give you the pleasure of beautiful blossom in the springtime, as well as the excitement of a rich harvest in the summer and autumn.

Top fruit

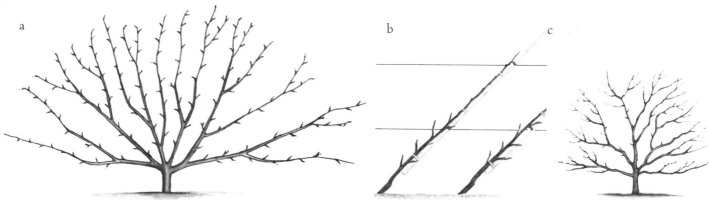

a

b

c

Fruit trees and bushes give a great deal of pleasure in the garden. There is the blossom in spring, which in the case of the apple and the peach, for example, is more than a match for any other flowering tree or shrub. Then there is the thrill of being able to gather your own fruit – bowls of raspberries and currants and baskets of apples and pears. What too can compare with juicy plums straight from the tree or a fragrant peach, faintly furry and warm in the sunshine?

There are fruit trees and bushes suitable for all gardens. It is simply a matter of tailoring the tree to your own particular needs. Let us start, in fact, with the tree fruits, or top fruits as they are sometimes called.

Types of trees

Bush trees are the most popular form for modern small gardens and they enable a considerable quantity of fruit to be grown. They have a trunk which is just 60cm (24in) high and they average 2.40m to 3m (8ft to 10ft) in height with a 3m to 3.60m (10ft to 12ft) spread. Fruits usually grown in bush form include apples, pears, peaches, plums and cherries. They are normally planted at least 3.60m (12ft) apart.

Cordon trees might have been developed with small gardens in mind, as no other form of tree allows so much fruit to be grown in such a small area. They have a single stem with very short side branches and can either be trained at an angle of 45° against wires in the open, or upright against house walls. Cordons grow to 3m (10ft) in length with a 45cm (18in) spread and are planted in rows with 60cm to

90cm (2ft to 3ft) between the trees, although they can be planted much further apart if you wish. Apples and pears are usually the only fruits grown in this form, but some nurseries can also offer cordon gooseberries and redcurrants.

Espalier, or horizontal trees, have a single central stem and two or three pairs of branches on either side which are trained on wires, either fixed to posts in the open or to a suitable wall. Apples and pears are the only trees grown by this method. The trees grow to 1.80m to 2.40m (6ft to 8ft) tall, depending on how many 'tiers' of branches are chosen, and they are planted 3.60m (12ft) apart.

Fan-shaped trees have short trunks and their branches trained on wires on a wall, or fence, in the form of the ribs of Japanese lady's fan. This type of training is normally reserved for the more exotic trees such as apricots, figs, peaches and nectarines as well as cherries, and plums. The average height of a fan tree on an outside wall is 3m (10ft) with a spread of 3m to 4.50m (10ft to 15ft). If more than one tree is grown, they should be 3.60m (12ft) apart.

Standard or half standard trees have the same shape as a bush, except that standards have 1.80m (6ft) trunks and a spread of 6m (20ft) and half standards have 1.20m (4ft) trunks and a spread of 4.50m (15ft). Apples, pears, plums and sweet cherries are all grown in this form, which is generally considered to be too large for ordinary gardens. However, what can be more pleasant than lazing on the lawn in the shade of a large apple tree? With more than one standard or half-standard tree, subsequent trees should be at least 6m (20ft) apart. But

d

e

Fruit trees can be tailored to suit the space available: a) fan-shaped b) cordon c) bush d) half-standard e) standard.

one tree is generally sufficient for most people and the problem of pollination can be solved by planting a smaller form of tree close by.

Pollination is normally carried out by the wind and insects. Some trees are described as self-fertile because it is simply a matter of insects transferring pollen from one flower to another on the same tree. Apricots, peaches, nectarines, sour cherries, some plums and all soft fruits are self-fertile. Other fruit trees require the pollen of trees of the same type but different varieties to ensure that the flowers develop into fruit. When buying your fruit trees, you should be able to find out from the nursery the most suitable and compatible trees for your area. Soil is rightly the basis

of success in growing fruit, but choice of plants follows very closely. No one would choose poor, stunted plants with unhealthy foliage, so take advantage of the disease-free fruit plants which nurserymen and scientists have produced.

Planting

The normal time for planting is sometime between November and March when the weather is mild and the soil is workable. Container-grown trees from garden centres can be planted at any time, provided they are watered regularly after planting.

The soil for fruit trees should be thoroughly broken up with a fork to a depth of 45cm (18in) and sufficient soil removed from the planting hole to accommodate the trees' roots comfortably. With bush and standard trees a stout stake should be hammered into the holes to support the tree before it is actually planted. Trim off any damaged roots with your secateurs. Then plant the tree so that the nursery soil mark on its trunk is at the same level as your garden soil. Fill in with good garden soil, or soil enriched by mixing it with well-rotted compost or peat. No artificial fertilizers are necessary at this point. Shake the tree from time to time to get the soil to settle around the roots and firm the soil around the trunk with your heel. Finally, use a 'tree-tie' to secure the trunk to the stake. If your tree is growing on the lawn, it is vital that a bare, weed-free circle of soil 1m (3ft) in diameter is maintained around the trunk for at least three years to enable the tree to become established and to prevent its having to compete with the grass for food and moisture.

Cordon, espalier and fan trees should have their supporting framework of wires set up before you get around to planting. For a row of cordons stretch wires between stout wooden or concrete posts at 30cm (12in), 90cm (3ft), 150cm (5ft) and 120cm (7ft) from the ground; for espalier trees stretch wires every 30cm (12in) to a height of 150cm to 180cm (5ft to 6ft), depending on the number of 'tiers'; for fans the wires should be secured to the wall or fence by pieces of ironmongery called 'vine eyes' so that you have a framework of horizontal wires at 23cm (9in) intervals to a height of 240cm (8ft).

Fruiting cherries can be beautiful as well as productive trees. They are among the first to blossom in the spring and the leaves turn to beautiful shades in the autumn.

Apple

Type of tree: Bush, standard, half-standard, cordon and espalier.

Pollination: At least two trees are necessary to produce fruit.

Aspect: Any. Early cooking apples can be grown on north facing walls.

Ideal soil: Well-drained ordinary soil which does not dry out excessively in summer.

Yield: 10 cordons will produce 20kg (44lb) of fruit; the same harvest can be obtained from one standard or half-standard, four bush trees or four espaliers.

Apple trees are hardy and flower in spring bearing fruit from July until the first frosts.

Planting and cultivation

The soil for apples can be made suitable by the addition of plenty of compost. For the first few years put down a moisture-retaining layer of compost or peat around the trees' roots in April and water copiously during dry spells. Every March top dress the soil around the spread of the branches with general fertilizer at the rate of $112g/m^2$ (4oz to a sq yd). In early June many of the smaller apples will be shed naturally from the tree. If the tree still appears to be bearing too heavy a crop, thin out the remainder and remove any inferior apples by cutting them from the tree with secateurs.

Harvesting

An apple is ready for picking if, when you cradle one in your hand and twist it gently, it comes away easily from the tree. Store the surplus which cannot be eaten within a few weeks by freezing or by wrapping the individual apples in newspaper and storing them in ventilated boxes or racks in a cool, humid place.

Pests and diseases

Aphids, codling moths (spray in mid-June and again in July with fenitrothion to kill caterpillars before they tunnel into the fruit), scab – blackish patches on fruit (spray with systemic fungicide at green bud, pink bud, petal fall and fruitlet stages).

Pruning

Crowded and crossing branches, also diseased or damaged shoots, can be removed from standard, half-standard and bush trees in winter. The idea is to produce an open centred tree which looks like a goblet-shaped wine glass. With cordon trees cut back the new growth on the side branches in September to one leaf beyond the original 'spurs' which the tree had when supplied by the nursery. If the autumn is mild, you may have to continue to prune in the same way to restrict the trees'

growth. If the spurs on mature cordons become overcrowded, thin or remove some of them completely in winter. The spurs on the horizontal branches of espalier trees are pruned in exactly the same way and at the same time as cordons. The extension growth of the horizontal branches, by which the tree increases in width, should be cut back by half to a bud (or leaf) in winter.

Above: Apple 'Laxton's fortune' bears a heavy crop. It makes a compact tree which is good for a smaller garden.

Below: The apple will be ready for picking if it comes away easily from the tree.

Pear

Type of tree: Bush, standard, half-standard, cordon and espalier.

Pollination: At least two trees are required to produce fruit.

Aspect: Sunny, or facing south or west. Sheltered from strong winds.

Ideal soil: Well-drained deep soil which does not dry out excessively in the summer months.

Yield: 10 cordons will produce 20kg (44lb) of fruit; a similar quantity of fruit can be obtained from one standard, or half-standard, four bush trees or four espaliers.

Planting and cultivation

Pears are just as easy to grow as apples if you choose the best possible varieties for your district. The famous Conference and William's Bon Chretien are the best choice for cold northern areas or chilly coastal districts. The soil should be improved by the addition of plenty of compost. Every March feed the soil around the spread of the trees' branches with general fertilizer at the rate of 112g/m² (4oz to a sq yd). In April surround the tree with a thick moisture-retaining layer of compost or damp peat. Pears are less tolerant of dry soil conditions than apples, and if the soil in June is not

sufficiently moist, the June drop of fruitlets can turn into a shedding of the entire crop.

Harvesting

Pears should not be allowed to become completely ripe on the tree if they are to be enjoyed at their best. Early varieties (August, September) should be cut from the tree while the fruit is still hard; mid season varieties (October, November) should be picked as soon as the fruit can be cupped in the hand and twisted gently free from the tree; late varieties (December onwards) can be harvested at the same stage of ripeness as mid season pears. The crop should be stored laid out in single layers on slatted shelves or boxes in a cool shed or garage. The fruits should not touch; neither should they be wrapped. Final ripening can be achieved by taking the fruit into a warm room for three days. Properly stored, pears will keep for months.

Pruning

Pears are pruned and trained in exactly the same way as apples. However they can stand much more severe cutting back, and in summer the pruning of cordons and espaliers may have to begin several weeks earlier.

Pests and diseases

Aphids, birds (do not allow fruit to remain too long on trees), pear scab (sooty blotches on leaves and fruit – spray with systemic fungicide at green bud, white bud, petal fall and fruitlet stages).

Apricot

Type of tree: Bush (suitable only in warm, sheltered gardens) and fan-trained.
Pollination: Self-fertile.
Aspect: Sunny or facing south or west.
Yield: 50 to 60 fruits annually.

Planting and cultivation

The soil can be improved if necessary by adding compost, but avoid excessive use of fertilizers as too rich soil encourages unnecessary leafy growth. The branches of fan trees should be secured loosely to a framework of wires. In cold districts fan trees can be trained against wires on one of the walls inside a greenhouse with a span of at least 3m (10ft). No heat is necessary. In March top dress the soil around the trees with general fertilizer at the rate of 112g/m² (4oz to a sq yd) under the spread of the branches. In April surround the trees with a thick layer of garden compost.

Although apricots are self-fertile, you are often better to do the job yourself by

dabbing the centre of each open flower in turn with an artist's brush.

Thinning the fruit is seldom necessary, but when the fruitlets are 2.5cm (1in) wide ensure that the crop is evenly spaced over the tree with 10cm (4in) between each fruit. Water the soil copiously whenever the weather is dry while the fruits are swelling to prevent them from splitting.

Harvesting

Thin the crop when the set is heavy, first at pea size to one fruitlet per cluster then again when the stone is formed.

Pick apricots as soon as they are ripe and well-coloured and can be pulled easily free of the tree.

Pruning and training

Bush trees need no regular pruning other than the removal of dead, diseased, weak and crossing branches in spring. With fan trees it is a good idea initially to pay a bit more and obtain a well-trained tree, as the basic shaping of the tree is somewhat beyond the scope of many weekend gardeners. However, assuming that you have a good tree, the side shoots should be pinched back to 7.5cm (3in) in May and June and the secondary side-shoots (sub-laterals) to one leaf. Crossing and crowded branches should also be removed. In autumn cut away those side shoots which have borne fruit and tie in the replacement growths from the base of the side shoots. If the 'ribs' of the fan grow beyond the space allotted in a greenhouse, cut them back to a strong side shoot.

Pests and diseases

Aphids, wasps and birds (protect with fine netting or plastic mesh netting), red spider mites (greenhouse trees have pale mottling on leaves – spray with malathion).

Opposite page, left: A variety of pear 'Louise Bonne of Jersey'.
Above: Twist the pear gently to free it from the tree.
Below: An ideal situation for apricots is on a sunny wall where they will benefit from the extra warmth absorbed by the bricks.

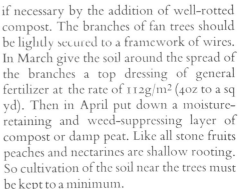

if necessary by the addition of well-rotted compost. The branches of fan trees should be lightly secured to a framework of wires. In March give the soil around the spread of the branches a top dressing of general fertilizer at the rate of $112g/m^2$ (4oz to a sq yd). Then in April put down a moisture-retaining and weed-suppressing layer of compost or damp peat. Like all stone fruits peaches and nectarines are shallow rooting. So cultivation of the soil near the trees must be kept to a minimum.

Although the trees are self-fertile, you are better to pollinate them yourself by dabbing the centre of each open flower in turn with an artist's brush. Plenty of water should be given whenever the soil dries out. Nectarines especially require copious watering while the fruits are swelling to prevent them from splitting. Thinning of the fruit is usually unnecessary, but if some are overcrowded, thin when the fruits are around 2.5cm (1in) in diameter to leave the remainder 23cm (9in) apart.

Harvesting
Pick the peaches and nectarines when the flesh around the stalks yields to gentle pressure from the fingers. The surplus crop will keep for a month if stored in a cool place.

Pruning and training
With bush trees, dead, damaged and crossing branches should be removed in May. On established bushes, older branches can be cut away too when they become unfruitful. With fan trees pinch back the sideshoots in May and June to the sixth leaf and the secondary side-shoots (sub-laterals) to one leaf. Crossing, crowded, and dead branches should also be removed.

In autumn, after picking the fruit, cut back each side-shoot which has borne fruit to its replacement, and secure the replacement shoots to the wires with twine. Once the extension growth from the 'ribs' of the fan reach their allotted space, treat them as if they too were fruiting side-shoots. If gaps appear in the fan structure, either through disease or neglect, fill them by retaining some of the fruited side-shoots and tying them to the wires.

Pests and diseases
Aphids, wasps and birds (protect with fine netting or plastic mesh netting), red spider mites (greenhouse trees have pale mottling on leaves – spray with malathion), leaf curl (leaves develop reddish blisters and drop from the tree – spray with lime sulphur at leaf-fall in autumn and repeat before the buds swell in mid-February).

Above: The peach 'Peregrine' which bears large fruit in mid-August.

Peaches and Nectarines
Type of tree: Bush or fan-trained.
Pollination: Self-fertile.
Aspect: Sunny, or facing south or west.
Ideal Soil: Any, provided it is well drained.
Yield: 50 to 60 fruits annually.

Planting and cultivation
Home-grown peaches are far superior to anything which you can buy from the shops; the fruit is large, juicy and pleasantly perfumed. A nectarine is simply a kind of peach with a smooth skin and with none of the characteristic peach fuzz. It is also more juicy with a slightly sharper flavour. Peaches can be grown outdoors as far north as the south of Scotland. Nectarines are less hardy and need the shelter of a sunny wall. Both peaches and nectarines are a splendid choice for a greenhouse with a span of at least 3m (10ft).

The trees should be planted in November in soil which has been improved

Plums, gages and damsons

Type of tree: Bush, half-standard, standard and fan trained (not damsons).

Pollination: All damsons, and some plums and gages are self-fertile. The remainder need the pollen from another variety flowering at the same time to produce a crop of fruit.

Aspect: Sunny, or facing east or west. The Victoria Plum will thrive on a north facing wall.

Ideal soil: Well-drained loam or clay containing a little lime.

Yield: One tree is enough for the average family.

Planting and cultivation

The trees should be planted in well-prepared soil in November or December. In March top dress the soil with general fertilizer at the rate of 112g/m² (4oz to a sq yd), under the spread of the branches. In April put down a thick moisture-retaining and weed-suppressing layer of compost. Soil cultivation should be avoided to prevent damage to the trees' surface roots. Thin the crop in June if necessary to take the weight off any obviously overladen branches. Leave the remainder 5cm (2in) apart.

Harvesting

Pick the fruit by the stalk to avoid bruising. Dessert plums and gages are best left on the tree until completely ripe; cooking plums and damsons should be gathered while still firm and under-ripe.

Pruning

Bush, standard and half-standard trees need little actual pruning apart from the removal of dead and crowded shoots. Young trees should be pruned in spring, while established trees are pruned in summer to enable the pruning cuts to heal and so prevent disease. Fan trees should have outward growing shoots removed in spring. In July all side-shoots which are not required should be pinched back to the sixth leaf. After the crop has been harvested, cut back by half all those shoots which were previously pinched back.

Pests and diseases

Aphids, birds and wasps (protect with fine netting or plastic mesh netting), bullfinches (little or no blossom – cover trees if possible with mesh netting in late winter and early spring).

Cherry (sour or cooking type)
Type of tree: Bush or fan.

Pollination: Self-fertile.

Aspect: Any, or north-facing.

Ideal Soil: Any, provided it is well drained.

Yield: One tree is sufficient for most families.

Planting and cultivation

There are two kinds of cherry tree: one which produces fruit for cooking and the other which produces sweet cherries. Unfortunately sweet cherries, even in fan-trained form, make very large trees which are unsuitable for most gardens. Another snag is that sweet cherries require the assistance of another cherry tree to give a crop of fruit. If that were not enough, birds have a great liking for sweet cherries, and protecting the crop in the garden is difficult. So all in all you are better to stick to a sour cherry. Plant your chosen type of tree in well-prepared soil between November and March, and maintain a 1m (3ft) circle of bare soil around its trunk for several years. In March top dress the soil under the spread of the branches with general fertilizer at the rate of 112g/m² (4oz to a sq yd). In April surround the tree with a thick moisture-retaining and weed-suppressing layer of compost.

Harvesting

The ripe fruit should be cut from the tree with secateurs or scissors to avoid damage to the shoots which can in turn cause disease.

Pruning and training

Bush cherry trees should be pruned once they have started to fruit by thinning out some of the shoots in the centre to allow in light and air. Dead wood, crowded and crossing branches should be cut away in

Above left: The plum 'Kirke's Blue' is in season in September.
Above top: 'Giant Prune' crops in mid-September.
Above: 'Bryanston' with its greenish-yellow skin also crops in September.

Opposite page, far left: The 'Merryweather' damson is good for bottling and freezing.
Opposite page, left: The 'Cambridge' gage is a dessert variety which crops in late summer.

spring after bud burst. With fan trees crowded branches and any dead wood should be cut away in spring. With cherries in general the rule is that the less pruning you do the better.

Pests and diseases

Aphids (cherry blackfly – spray with formothion or dimethoate immediately after flowering).

Fig

Type of tree: bush or fan.
Pollination: Self-fertile.
Aspect: Sunny or south-facing.
Ideal soil: Fertile and well-drained.
Yield: One tree is sufficient for most families.

Planting and cultivation

Figs can be grown successfully outdoors in Britain south of the Trent. Elsewhere you are best to grow a bush tree in a 25cm (10in) diameter clay pot and to stand this in a greenhouse. In fact even outdoors you should grow your tree in a pot, as the restriction of the pot on the fig's roots encourages it to bear fruit.

March is the best month for planting. The pots can either be filled with good garden soil or John Innes No. 3 compost.

Outdoors, choose a 30cm (12in) diameter clay pot and sink this up to its rim in the garden soil in the chosen position. Your fig can either remain as a bush, growing to little more than 1.20m (4ft) high or you can sink the pot close to a sunny wall and fan train the branches against wires at 23cm (9in) intervals from the ground to a height of 1.80m (6ft).

Figs need plenty of water during the late spring and summer months, but feeding initially is not required. After three years, however, you can give a feed in spring and summer with a liquid general fertilizer.

Harvesting

Gather the figs when they are soft and the skin has just begun to split.

Pruning and training

With bush trees all frost-damaged or twisted shoots can be cut away in early April. If you wish to train a tree to a fan shape, cut the branches to the basic shape in early April. At the end of June, cut off the ends of side-shoots at the fourth leaf to encourage the formation of new and further fruit-bearing side-shoots. In July choose new shoots which will grow parallel to the wall and, using bamboo canes as splints, tie them into the required positions.

Pests and diseases: Virtually trouble-free.

Soft fruit

Every garden no matter how small has room for soft fruits. Strawberries and even a clump of raspberries can be grown among the flowers. The canes of blackberries and loganberries can be trained on walls and fences. Currants and goosberries can take the place of shrubs and look equally attractive.

Strawberry
Planting and cultivation

There are three kinds of strawberry; the summer fruiting varieties, the perpetual fruiting varieties and the alpines. They can be planted in spring, late summer or autumn. Strawberries do best in a sunny position in soil which has been well prepared by the addition of plenty of peat. However no artificial fertilizers are required. Tread the soil firm and allow to settle for a few weeks before planting. The plants should be set out 45cm (18in) apart each way so that the crown of each plant is level with the soil surface. Water the plants if the weather is dry, and should any plants be lifted by frost, dig them up and replant.

The runners from summer fruiting varieties should be cut off close to the parent plants when they appear, unless you wish to use them to increase your stock of plants. Perpetual fruiting varieties do not normally produce many runners, but those that do bear flowers and fruit should be retained. Alpines do not have runners.

Once the flowers appear, surround the plants with a thick layer of peat to keep the fruit clean. Then after fruiting, feed the plants with a tomato fertilizer rich in potash. Summer fruiting varieties should have all their leaves removed after fruiting to prevent disease. Perpetual fruiting strawberries should have their leaves removed in autumn. Alpines need no such treatment. The entire stock of plants should be renewed every third year from a reputable source and a fresh strawberry bed established in a new spot. Alpines can either be divided in March, as you would do with an herbaceous plant, and the best pieces replanted, or you can raise new plants from seed.

Pests and diseases

Aphids, grey mould, slugs and birds (protect with netting).

Currants, black, red or white

Size: 1.20m to 1.50m high by 90cm (4ft to 5ft by 3ft).
Pollination: Self-fertile.
Aspect: Sunny or partial shade.
Ideal soil: Any, provided it is moisture-retentive and well-drained.

Planting and cultivation

The soil should be well prepared by digging and working in plenty of compost or peat. Planting can be carried out any time between November and March, but the earlier the better. The bushes should be spaced at least 1.20m (4ft) apart. Blackcurrants should be set in the soil so that the bushes are 5cm (2in) deeper than they were at the nursery. Look for the soil mark on the stems before you plant. Redcurrants and whitecurrants are grown quite differently from the black varieties and con-

'Talisman' is a popular strawberry—grown in a good situation it will produce a heavy crop.

bushes with open centres which let in light and air.

After planting red or white currants, all branches should be cut back to 5cm to 7.5cm (2in to 3in) to outward facing buds. In future winters cut back the leading shoots by half. In February cut back the side-shoots to two to three buds.

Pests and diseases

Aphids; blackcurrant gall mites (buds in winter swell up and wither in spring – remove and burn infected growth. Spray with lime sulphur or malathion when the flowers first open and repeat three weeks later); birds (cover bushes with netting to protect buds in winter and fruit in summer).

Gooseberry
Size: 1.20m by 90cm (4ft by 3ft).
Pollination: Self-fertile.
Aspect: Sunny or partial shade.
Ideal soil: Any, provided it is well drained. It is tolerant of chalky soils.

Planting and cultivation
Gooseberries can be planted any time during late autumn or winter in soil which has been prepared by digging in plenty of compost or peat. The bushes should be set in the soil a little higher than the nursery soil mark on the stems, and they should be spaced at least 1.20m (4ft) apart. In March feed them with general fertilizer at the rate of 112g (4oz) to each bush. In April surround the bushes with a thick layer of compost or moist peat. Care must be taken when weeding not to damage the roots which are close to the surface. Chemical weed control is often the best.

Harvesting
Pick the first fruit for cooking when the gooseberries are still firm. Fruit for eating should be picked when soft and fully ripe.

Pruning and training
In winter the leading shoots are cut back by half and in February or March the side-shoots are cut back to two or three buds. Some thinning out of the centre of the bush may also be necessary to let in light and air.

Pests and diseases
Aphids; sawflies; American gooseberry mildew (powdery deposit on leaves and fruit becomes brown – cut away infected shoots in autumn and spray in spring with a benomyl fungicide at regular intervals); birds (bullfinches eat fruit buds in winter – cover with netting).

Above top: Take care not to damage the fruit when harvesting.
Above: White currants grow on strong upright bushes bearing heavy crops of berries.

sequently the bushes are planted at the same level as at the nursery, or slightly higher.

In March feed each bush with 168g (6oz) of general fertilizer and, in April, surround the bushes with a thick layer of compost or damp peat to keep down weeds and to retain moisture. The roots of currants are close to the soil surface and care must be taken when weeding not to damage them. You could consider using a chemical method of weed control.

Harvesting
Pick the individual berries one at a time if you want to enjoy them at their best. Otherwise wait for two weeks after the fruit has completely coloured before cutting away the bunches with scissors.

Pruning and training
After planting cut back all the shoots of blackcurrants to within 2.5cm (1in) of soil level. In the first autumn after planting cut down the weakest blackcurrant shoots to soil level. In future years when the bushes are established, cut about a quarter of the oldest branches of blackcurrants down to soil level annually in autumn to encourage renewal growth. Also, attempt to produce

Raspberries

Size: 1.20m to 2m by 45cm (4ft to 6ft by 18in).
Pollination: Self-fertile.
Aspect: Sunny or partial shade.
Ideal Soil: Slightly acid, fertile soil which is well drained.

Planting and cultivation

There are two types of raspberries: summer fruiting and autumn fruiting. Both should be planted between November and March in soil enriched with compost. Plant so that the root system is about 7.5cm (3in) deep and the individual canes are about 45cm (18in) apart. Subsequent rows of raspberries should be at least 1.20m (4ft) apart.

Feed in March with general fertilizer at the rate of 112g (4oz) to 1m (1yd) of row. In April surround the canes with a moisture-retaining and weed-suppressing layer of compost or peat. Weeds should be kept down with either a hoe, used carefully to avoid damaging the roots, or a chemical weedkiller.

Summer raspberries need some support to prevent their toppling over in windy weather. This is best provided by tying the canes to wires strained horizontally between stout wooden posts at 1.05m (3½ft) and 1.5m (5ft) from the ground. Autumn fruiting raspberries rarely exceed 1.20m (4ft) in height and can be grown without support.

Harvesting

Pick when the fruits are well coloured and easily removed from the stalks.

Pruning and training

All newly planted canes should be cut back to 15cm to 30cm (6in to 12in) after planting. In the first summer after planting neither summer nor autumn fruiting raspberries require any pruning. All the canes of autumn fruiting raspberries should be cut to the ground annually in February. Summer fruiting raspberries are treated differently. The canes of summer fruiting raspberries are cut away immediately these have borne fruit and the new season's growth of canes are tied in to take their place. With both autumn and summer fruiting raspberries you should limit the number of canes arising from one plant to six.

Pests and diseases

Aphids, and raspberry beetle (spray with derris, fenitrothion or malathion when fruit turns pink).

Above: Raspberries do not travel well, so it is possible to pick from the garden berries of a quality which cannot be found in the shops. Below left: Gooseberry 'Careless' has pale fruit with a good flavour.

Blackberries and hybrid berries (loganberry and boysenberry)

Size: Spread of 3.60m to 5.40m (12ft to 18ft).
Pollination: Self-fertile.
Aspect: Any.
Ideal soil: Slightly acid, fertile soil which is well-drained. Blackberries and hybrid berries are vigorous and exceptionally spiny, hardy cane fruits. The fruits can be used for dessert, bottling, tarts, jam and wine.

Planting and cultivation

It is worth making an effort to enrich the soil for blackberries and other hybrid berries with compost as a single plant can yield enormous quantities of fruit. The other essential is to prepare some sort of framework of supporting wires on a wall or fence. Alternatively you can strain wires horizontally at 90cm, 1.20m and 1.50m (3ft, 4ft and 5ft) from the ground between posts so that you have a framework at least 4.50m (15ft) long. Planting can take place anytime between November and March.

Harvesting

Pick the fruits when they are well-coloured and come away easily from the stalks.

Pruning and training

After planting, cut the existing canes to 23cm (9in) from soil level. In future years cut away all the old canes after fruiting and tie in the new season's canes to take their place.

Pests and diseases

Aphids and raspberry beetle (spray with derris, fenitrothion or malathion when the fruit first shows colour).

Blueberry

Size: 1.20m by 90cm (4ft by 3ft).
Pollination: Self-fertile, but two bushes ensure a better crop.
Aspect: Sunny or partial shade, sheltered from cold winds.
Ideal soil: Acid soil which retains moisture.

Planting and cultivation

The blueberry is an American fruit and a relative of our native bilberry. However, in terms of fruit it is far superior and makes delicious jam, jelly and wine. The soil should be prepared by adding plenty of peat and the bushes should be planted between November and March, spacing them 90cm (3ft) apart. If your garden soil is alkaline, you could grow blueberries in 30cm (12in) diameter tubs containing John Innes No. 3 compost and some peat. In March feed the bushes with 56g (2oz) of general fertilizer. In April surround them with a thick layer of damp peat. If you have to water the bushes, try to use rainwater, not water from the tap.

Harvesting

Pick the berries while still firm for jam making; for other dessert purposes allow them to become soft and fully ripe.

Pruning and training

Pruning is unnecessary. However some of the older wood can be cut away in winter once the bushes have started cropping.

Pests and diseases

Birds (it is vital to protect the crop from birds when the fruit is ripened with fine plastic netting). Otherwise, completely trouble-free.

Below left: The loganberry is ideal for all kinds of culinary uses: stewing, jam-making, jelly-making, bottling, and wine-making. Below right: The cultivated blackberry which makes delicious jam and wine.

Melon
Sowing and cultivation
The best type of melon for growing in Britain is the cantaloupe. It is sufficiently hardy to be grown in a cold frame or under cloches in mild districts. Sow the seeds in 7.5cm (3in) diameter peat pots containing peat-based compost in April or May, and place the pots in a warm dark spot until the seeds germinate, normally in around five days. Then remove the pots into the light and keep them in a sunny spot indoors until early June. The seedlings can then be set outdoors 90cm (3ft) apart on specially prepared soil in a sunny spot.

Melons like soil rich in organic matter, so at each planting position take out a section of soil the width and depth of your spade and replace it with an equal mixture of soil and compost. Once planted the melons should be covered with large, rigid plastic cloches. In cold districts melons are best grown in a frame. In this case plant two or three melon plants in a compost-filled growing bag in the frame. Pinch out the growing point of the plants when they have four rough edged leaves to encourage side-shoots to develop. In a frame, train two of these shoots on either side of the

growing bag. Under cloches train two shoots horizontally on either side of the plant. Fruit will be borne on each of the four main shoots. Grow just one melon on each shoot and pinch off its growing point two leaves beyond the fruit. When the flowers appear, leave the end pieces off the cloches and the frame slightly open so that insects can do the necessary pollinating.

The plants should be watered daily and liquid feeds should be given every ten days when the fruits are walnut size. When the melons are tennis ball sized, place them on pieces of wood, tile or slate to keep them clean. When the melon gives off a pleasant scent and the stalk starts to crack beside the fruit, you will known that the fruit is almost ripe. At this point stop watering and increase the amount of air reaching the plants.

Harvesting
A melon is ready for harvesting when its skin yields slightly to pressure from the thumb at the opposite end from the stalk. At this point the melon can be cut away from the plant.

Pests and diseases
Virtually none if the plants are correctly grown in conditions suitable to their variety.

Above left: A large melon such as this one needs to be held away from the ground to keep it clean and to prevent it from breaking off.

Above right: Pollinating by hand is an alternative to pollination by insects. Strip the petals off a male flower; insert core into female flower to transfer pollen.

The plants should be set out 60cm to 90cm (2ft to 3ft) apart so that new shoots are just showing above the soil. Tread the soil firmly around the roots. The first season you are best to concentrate on building up the strength of the plants and no stalks should be pulled.

Plenty of water should be given in dry spells. In late April cover the bed with a thick layer of well-rotted compost and in July, when the final harvest has been made, give the bed an annual dressing of general fertilizer at the rate of 168g/m² (6oz to a sq yd).

Never allow flowers to form. Any which do appear should be snapped off when first seen. An established rhubarb bed will give good results over a number of years before it requires major attention. When the annual harvest is of poorer quality, the bed can be revitalized in winter by lifting the roots, dividing them with a spade and replanting the best pieces.

Harvesting
Rhubarb should be pulled by grasping the stems low down. Do not snap the stems away from the crown as the pieces left behind rot and cause damage to the rootstock.

Pests and diseases
Crown rot (shoots are thin and discoloured, rootstock develops a blackish cavity – lift and burn as there is no cure).

Above: Rhubarb is in season from March until the end of June. Below right: The grape vine has attractive leaves, and this variety 'Brandt' fruits well in a good year.

Rhubarb
Planting and cultivation
The beauty of rhubarb is that it provides desserts early in the year before other fruits are ready. It is in season from March until the end of June. The crop is produced from rootstocks, or crowns, which are best planted in March in well prepared soil to which plenty of compost has been added.

Vine, grape

Spread: 1.20m to 6m (4ft to 20ft) depending on the method of cultivation.
Pollination: Self-fertile.
Aspect: Sunny.
Ideal soil: Well-drained soil enriched with compost.

Planting and cultivation (and pruning)

Growing grapes in many parts of Britain is no more difficult than growing raspberries. However you must obtain a variety, be it French, German, American, Russian or a British hybrid which is suitable for outdoor growing. A vine can be trained on a house wall, and it looks very decorative, as well as providing fruit. You can also grow vines in a row in the open ground and have your own vineyard.

First, let us consider a vine against a wall. Plant your chosen variety between November and February against a sunny, sheltered wall in soil enriched with compost.

The first year allow the vine to grow freely and tie the shoots to a tall bamboo cane. In the autumn, select two strong shoots and cut them back by half their length. All other shoots should be cut away at the base. You can then put up two parallel wires 60cm (2ft) apart on the wall vertically initially, then horizontally secured to pieces of ironmongery called 'vine eyes'. The vine shoots, hereafter called 'rods' should then be lightly tied to the wires. In future years these main stems or rods should be allowed to grow freely, but cut back each autumn half of the season's extension growth. The side shoots from the main stems should also be cut back in autumn, after harvesting, to two buds. In spring, when shoots form on these short spurs, the best two shoots should be retained and the others removed. In early summer pinch back the sideshoots arising from the spurs to two leaves beyond a bunch of fruit. Allow just one bunch of fruit to each side-shoot.

With vines in the open stretch wires horizontally at 60cm (2ft) and 1.20m (4ft) from the ground between stout posts. The vines can then be planted in soil prepared earlier by digging in plenty of compost. Allow 1.20m (4ft) between each vine and provide each one with a stout bamboo cane to support the first year's growth. In the autumn select the two strongest shoots and cut back to 1.2m (4ft). Then tie them to the lower wire on either side of the vine. The other shoots should be cut away at two buds from the base. The following year allow one bunch of grapes to each side shoot and stop the growth at two leaves beyond this point.

Treat the extension growths on the rods as if they too were side-shoots. The buds on the base of the vine will send up new shoots which should be secured to the cane and topmost wire. In autumn cut away the rods which have borne fruit at two buds from the base and shorten and tie in the best two new shoots to take their place. In April give vines in the open and against walls a top dressing of 112g (4oz) of general fertilizer and a thick moisture-retaining and feeding layer of compost. Water copiously in dry spells.

Harvesting

Leave the grapes on the vines until they are completely ripe. Then cut them from the vine with secateurs.

Pests and diseases

Scale insects (plants sticky and sooty); birds; powdery mildew (cut out severely infected shoots in autumn, spray with a benomyl fungicide during wet summers).

An old-established vinery with the fruit ripening under glass shows how a variety will grow well if suitable conditions are ensured.

THE SPOILERS

Without proper treatment and control, pests and disease can rob you of the successes you have gained in your garden, and lay waste your year's efforts.

Pests & Diseases

Once you have spent hours of hard work and given your garden a great deal of loving care it is disheartening to find that pests and diseases have robbed you of the pleasure of seeing perfect plants, fruits and vegetables. So it is vital to identify your enemies and to prevent their destroying your efforts.

Some pests are difficult to isolate because they are able to change their form, and with their new phase go in for a fresh mode of attack. For instance, you get the egg, then the caterpillar and finally the butterfly (or moth). Other pests are not quite so devious, but whether in their young or adult stage, aphids can cause a great deal of damage.

The more you know about your enemies the better chance you will have of getting rid of them. Caterpillars, earwigs and weevils chew their food, thus reducing leaves to tatters. Greenfly and capsids prefer to pierce plant tissues and suck the sap. As if this damage were not bad enough, the activities of these pests make the plants susceptible to secondary diseases.

Good garden practice is the best way of keeping pests under control. By digging in winter you expose the pupae and grubs as well as horrors such as cutworms, leather jackets and wireworm to birds and frost. The rotation of crops in the vegetable plot prevents a build up of the diseases which affect certain plants. Hoeing not only kills weeds, but it removes the refuge for such pests as soil caterpillars and cutworms. Feeding plants regularly keeps them growing strongly and able to ward off attacks from pests and diseases and it is the weaker plants which are most liable to succumb. By keeping the garden tidy and free from plant refuse you will deny slugs and snails a valuable source of food and shelter. You will also eliminate a breeding ground for other pests. You should also encourage your friends in the garden, the starlings which feed on pests such as leatherjackets and the robins which like all sorts of grubs. Some insects, too, such as ladybirds, are especially useful since they feed on aphids.

Biological control of pests and diseases is everyone's ideal, but to be effective you would have to persuade all of your neighbours to do likewise. Chemical control, both natural (pyrethrum, for example) and synthetic, is perfectly safe and sensible, provided that you always follow the recommendations made by the manufacturers. Most plant pests are killed by spraying either with a contact spray, or a systemic insecticide. A contact spray kills the pest either by hitting it directly or by poisoning its food. A systemic insecticide is absorbed by the plant's system and kills the sucking type of insects. This is why the modern systemic insecticides are the best choice for killing aphids. For pests in the soil, granular insecticides have been developed which can simply be sprinkled around plants to give protection. Similarly poison in the form of pellets can be put down to keep slugs and snails away from such delicacies as strawberries and melons.

For the sake of the environment and for the delicate balance of nature, treating pests and diseases should be kept at a sensible level. Also it is of the utmost importance that any spraying and syringing operations are carried out carefully.

Aphids (greenfly, blackfly, also cream, grey, pink and brown)

Symptoms

Some leaves stunted and discoloured; sticky honeydew and presence of ants; sooty mould.

Treatment

Spray with a systemic insecticide on ornamental plants, trees and fruit trees. Use a vegetable insecticide on vegetables. If ladybirds are present, use one of the new *selective* systemic insecticides, for example, one containing Pirimicarb which will only attack the aphids.

Beetles and weevils

Symptoms: Holes in brassica seedling leaves, including those of radish, swede and turnip. Scalloped edges to pea and bean leaves and also those of polyanthus. Apple fruit buds eaten with no fruit resulting.

Treatment: Spray with either systemic or vegetable insecticide.

Below: The aphids presence is obvious by stickiness on the plant and the presence of ants.
Below bottom: Regular holes around the leaf edge are typical of the presence of weevils.

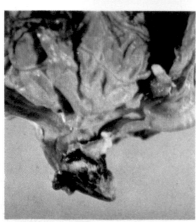

Birds

Symptoms: Leaves of lettuce or seedlings eaten down to ground level; flower buds eaten with no fruit resulting.

Treatment: Cover crop with fine plastic netting when the fruit or vegetable is ripe and hang brightly-coloured plastic bags or pieces of tin foil strung together

Black spot

Symptoms: Yellowed areas and black blotches on rose leaves which fall prematurely.

Treatment: Rake up all leaves in winter and burn. Spray with a systemic fungicide during spring and summer. Better still grow resistant varieties.

Botrytis (grey mould)

Symptoms: Leaves, stems and fruit covered with fluffy grey mould. Fruit rots.

Treatment: Spray with a fungicide containing benomyl. Keep the atmosphere in frames and greenhouses drier, and outside avoid splashing water on stems, leaves and flowers.

Cabbage root fly

Symptoms: Maggots eat brassica roots. The plants turn bluish, wilt and often die.

Treatment: There is no cure as such, but the pests can be prevented by scattering the granules of a soil insecticide around each plant as a single dose between April and August.

Capsid bugs

Symptoms: Flattish insects, light brown or greenish in colour produce a speckled brownish pinhole appearance on leaves, shoots and fruit. The blooms of dahlias and chrysanthemums develop a lop-sided appearance.

Treatment: Spray with a systemic insecticide or fenitrothion, according to the instructions of the manufacturers.

Carrot fly

Symptoms: Maggots in carrots.

Treatment: There is no actual cure, but you can take preventative steps by delaying sowing to May and burying all thinnings on the compost heap. You can also sprinkle soil insecticide along the seed drills before sowing and give a further dose in early May, early August and in September if necessary.

Caterpillars

Symptoms: Holes eaten out of leaves in spring and summer.

Treatment: Spray vegetables and fruit with a vegetable insecticide; spray ornamental plants with systemic insecticide.

Clubroot

Symptoms: Brassicas become stunted; roots are swollen.

Treatment: None, but prevent by ensuring that the soil is rich in organic matter and well limed to prevent the acidic conditions which favour club root fungus. The planting holes can be dusted with mercurous chloride (Calomel dust) when transplanting as a preventative measure.

Cutworms and leatherjackets

Symptoms: Plants collapse with stems eaten through at, or below ground level.

Treatment: Hoe regularly to expose the pests to birds, frogs and toads. As a preventative measure soil insecticide can be sprinkled around seedlings and plants.

Damping off

Symptoms: Seedlings collapse at ground level.

Treatment: Use only sterile seed compost when raising plants in clean trays and pots. Watering with Cheshunt Compound can prevent the infection from spreading.

Earwigs

Symptoms: Ragged looking foliage and chewed flower petals, especially on dahlias and chrysanthemums.

Treatment: Drench the plants with an insecticide.

Grubs

Symptoms: Holes in the fruit of apples, pears and plums, peas, raspberries and blackberries.

Treatment: Spray apples and pears mid-June and mid-July with fenitrothion or systemic insecticide to kill codling moth maggots. Spray at petal fall and again ten days later with systemic insecticide to kill apple sawflies. The pea moth can be avoided by sowing in early March (or by early April in Scotland) or otherwise spray with insecticide at evening when flowers just open and repeat ten days later. For maggots in pears (pear midge) spray with a systemic insecticide when the flower buds are white. Maggots of the raspberry beetle can be prevented by spraying with derris, fenitrothion or malathion when the fruit colours.

Leaf Hoppers

Symptoms: Mottled patches with a characteristic residue on the undersides of leaves of trees, shrubs and ornamentals, especially roses.

Treatment: Spray with either systemic insecticide or spray with vegetable insecticide.

Leaf Miners

Symptoms: Irregular channels or whitish blisters on the leaves of celery, chrysanthemum, cineraria, holly and lilac.

Treatment: Celery – spray early May, June and July; chrysanthemum – spray at 14 day intervals all summer; holly and lilac spray late May. In all cases use a systemic insecticide.

Mice

Symptoms: Beans, peas and bulbs fail to produce growth despite adequate precautions.

Treatment: Bait and set traps beneath cloches. Plant bulbs of lilies inside guards of fine wire netting, and this will prevent the mice from attacking and devouring the bulbs.

Onion Fly

Symptoms: Whitish maggots burrow into the base of young bulbs, causing wilting and loss of plants.

Treatment: There is no cure, but sow seeds in late summer or early winter to avoid the pest. Alternatively, use onion 'sets' which are not affected. Chemical control can be achieved by sprinkling soil insecticide along the drills before sowing or along rows of seedlings when they are 3cm to 5cm (1in to 2in) high.

Peach leaf curl

Symptoms: Leaf curl with crimson blistering at first followed by a thickening of the foliage which then turns white before falling. Trees affected – almond, peach and nectarine.

Treatment: Spray with lime sulphur when the leaves are dropping in the autumn and repeat again at bud burst, generally in mid-February.

Powdery mildew

Symptoms: Upper and lower leaf surfaces are covered in a white deposit which may cause distortion.

Treatment: Roses should be sprayed regularly with a rose fungicide to keep them free from infection. Other plants should be sprayed with a benomyl fungicide.

Red spider mite

Symptoms: Microscopic mites cause pale mottling on the leaves of greenhouse trees and plants and outdoors in summer on roses, runner beans, strawberries and other plants.

Treatment: Keep a humid atmosphere in greenhouses, otherwise spray with a systemic insecticide.

Root aphid

Symptoms: Whitish mealy pests on roots of lettuce cause the plants to wilt.

Treatment: Surround the plants with a light sprinkling of soil insecticide.

Rust

Symptoms: Black or rust coloured spores on the undersides of leaves of antirrhinum, carnation, hollyhock, mint, plum and roses. Leaves fall prematurely.

Treatment: Spray roses with rose fungicide regularly. Other plants spray with liquid copper fungicide and repeat weekly if necessary.

Scale insects

Symptoms: Tiny shell-like insects on fruit trees, ornamental trees and shrubs and greenhouse pot plants. Sooty moulds on stems.

Treatment: Spray with a systemic insecticide three times at 14-day intervals.

Slugs and snails

Symptoms: Leaves chewed; faint silvery trails around plants.

Treatment: Keep the garden free from decaying matter. Surround susceptible seedlings and plants with a layer of moist peat. As a last resort, put down slug bait.

Thrips (thunderflies)

Symptoms: Silver mottling and severe distortion of shoots on greenhouse plants, gladioli, onions and peas.

Treatment: Spray with systemic insecticide or a vegetable insecticide.

Wireworm

Symptoms: Yellowish or brown thread-like grubs which feed on root crops.

Treatment: Soil should be dusted with soil insecticide or Gamma-BHC. Potatoes and carrots should not be grown until the pests are eliminated. Often a serious pest in new gardens; cultivation exposes the wireworms to birds.

Below: These red eggs will soon hatch the red spider mite, the cause of shrivelled leaves and defoliated plants. Below bottom: Wireworms are usually brown or brownish red and can do great damage to the roots of vegetables and flowers.

Index

Pictures supplied by

B. Alfieri 31(T),65(T),78(T).
Amateur Gardening 22(B),30.
D. Arminson 21(B),27(L),36(T),47(c).
Barnaby's Picture Library 62(T),70,74(T).
P. Becker 87(T).
Bevilacqua 47(T).
Steve Bicknell 67.
P. Booth 52(R),87(T).
R. J. Corbin 7,8,10,15,17,18,35(T & BR),43,44,46(T),54(B),55(T),
56,57(BL & BR),58,60(T),61(T),66(T),73(B).
P. Dowell 66(B).
J. Downward 26(R).
G. Drury 64(B).
Alan Duns 55(B).
Valerie Finnis 23(B),25(T),64(T),83.
Brian Furner 49(B),50(B),51,57(T),60(B),81,82(T).
P. Genereux 31(BR).
S. Grubb 31(BL).
M. Hadfield 40(L).
Grant Heilman 59(R).
P. Hunt 25(B),38.
G. Hyde 29(T),35(BL),40(R),62(B),84(T),86(B),87(B).
I.C.I. 86(T).
L. Johns 13,41.
Agnete Lampe 2/3.
E. Megson 71.
Ministry of Agriculture & Fisheries 86(C).

Murphy Chemical Co. 85(B).
National Vegetable Research Station 85(T).
Natural History Photographic Agency 84(B).
Maurice Nimmo 39.
Roger Phillips 49(T).
Picturepoint 45(T).
R. Procter 65(B).
J. Proctor 76(R).
Kim Sayer 6.
D. Smith 68,74(BL & BR),75,76(L),78(B),79(T),80.
Harry Smith Horticultural Photographic Library 12,20,21(T),
22(T),23(T),27(R),28,29(BR),33,34,37,45(B),47(B),48,50(T),53,
54(T),59(L),61(B),72(B),77,79(B),80,82(B).
V. Stevenson 26(L)
Transworld 42.
D. Wildridge 24.
D. Woodland 29(BL).
Joyce Wreford 5.